WHILE MEN SLEPT...

... his enemy came and sowed tares
among the wheat
Matthew 13:25

KAREN FRAZIER ROMERO

Order this book online at www.trafford.com
or email orders@trafford.com

Most Trafford titles are also available at major online book retailers.

Scripture quotations are taken from the King James Version
Expositors Study Bible. Copyright © 2005.

Printed in the United States of America.

ISBN: 978-1-4907-2890-2 (sc)
ISBN: 978-1-4907-2889-6 (e)

Trafford rev. 03/03/2014

 www.trafford.com

North America & international
toll-free: 1 888 232 4444 (USA & Canada)
fax: 812 355 4082

Contents

To the past Watchmen who persistently warned the flock . . .
I personally accept the challenge of Justin Fulton given in 1888 . . .
"Somebody will catch this inspiration, and
become a trumpeter of great truth."

And to the Lord Who encouraged me to go forth with this work:
"Declare ye among the nations, and publish, and set up a standard;
Publish, and conceal not."
Jeremiah 50:2

Chapter One

THE GREATEST LOVE STORY OF ALL TIME

The material presented in this book shows the greatest conspiracy ever conceived by mankind when inspired by Satan. Anyone who reads it will forever look at the world in a completely different manner. If your faith is not grounded on God's Word and what Jesus Christ came to do when He died on the Cross for the sins of humanity, then it may be quite disturbing and could potentially even cause paranoia. That is why every book written by these hands strives to declare the amazing love story of God when He sent His Son Jesus to offer redemption to humanity. Please take this chapter very seriously and if you have not yet become **"born again"** of the Spirit making you a new creation in Christ Jesus, then now is your opportunity! Not only will you receive the gift of Eternal Life, but you will also rest peacefully at night despite the evil surrounding us each and every day.

Jesus says to Nicodemus, one of the religious leaders of Israel, in **John 3:3, "Except a man be born again, he cannot see the Kingdom of Heaven."** Nicodemus thought he was saved because he was a very religious man, but Jesus explains to him that he was once born of water at his physical birth and he now must be born again of the Spirit by accepting by faith that Jesus was the Son of God sent to redeem the whole world of sin.

You see, God created for man a perfect world without sin and death. It was the temptation of Satan in the Garden of Eden which tempted Adam to sin against God and consequently brought sin and death into the world. In **Genesis 3:15**, God promised to send a Redeemer who would crush the head of the serpent, which is Satan, thereby destroying him! God spoke directly to Satan after he caused Adam's fall and said, **"And I will put enmity between you and the woman, and between your seed and her Seed; it shall bruise your head** (the destruction of Satan), **and you shall bruise His heel** (the sufferings of Jesus on the Cross)."

Romans 6:23 says, **"For the wages of sin is death, but the Gift of God is Eternal Life through Jesus Christ our Lord."** *Jesus was that promised Gift!* Every person born after the time of Adam was born with a sin nature. **Romans 5:12** states, **"Wherefore by one man sin entered the world, and death by sin; and so death passed upon all men, for that all have sinned."** I realize that it does not seem very fair, but it's true! Because Jesus was conceived of the Holy Spirit and not by man, He was not born with the sin nature. He also remained perfect and completely free of sin the entire time He walked this Earth. The Bible says in **2 Corinthians 5:21** that He **"knew no sin,"** even though He **"was in all points tempted, like as we are . . . (Hebrews 4:15)."** Therefore, when He went to the Cross to die for the penalty of *our* sin, God was able to resurrect Him three days later! Had Jesus sinned even one time, God would not have raised Him from the dead because **". . . the wages of sin is death."** Jesus defeated sin, death and Satan, who brought sin and death into this world at the Fall of Man. The blood that He shed gave man fellowship with God again and made Eternal Life in Heaven possible for all who would put their faith in His sacrifice.

Everyone will one day stand before God as a judge. He may ask why you deserve to enter into Heaven. If the answer is because of your own goodness or that because you belonged to a particular religion or Church denomination, then He will say, **". . . I never knew you, depart from Me . . . (Matthew 7:23)."** The answer should be, *"I have put my faith in your only Son, Jesus, Who paid the penalty of sin which I could not pay on my own."*

Some think that if they are a "good person" that they will make Heaven upon death. Sadly, I too reasoned that same thought process. The darkness of sin had concealed the wickedness of my own heart. It was not until I accepted the **"light of the world,"** Jesus Christ, into my life that I began to see the sin that abounded in my heart. Many believe that as long as the "good outweighs the bad," then they are safe from the fires of Hell. God created the Moral Law, which was given to Moses, to define sin and Jesus was the *only* one who ever kept the law perfectly. **James 2:10 says, "For whosoever shall keep the whole Law, and yet offend in one point, he is guilty of all."** And **Romans 3:23** states, **"For all have sinned and come short of the Glory of God."** Thank God our righteousness will be based on Jesus' perfection and not our own! God's Word also states in **Ephesians 2:8-9, "For by Grace are you saved through faith; and that not of yourselves, it is the Gift of God: not of works, lest any man should boast."** It is not possible to work for or earn our salvation; it is a gift from God! All we need to do is put our faith in what Jesus already accomplished for us on the Cross and keep it there! It is really that simple!

What if you go to Church regularly and follow their laws; will you then be eligible for salvation? Again, there is nothing we can *do* to work for our salvation including Church attendance or following certain laws, rituals or sacraments. The Bible is very clear on this fact and God's Word should be our benchmark for truth. **Galatians 2:21** says, **"I do not frustrate the Grace of God: for if righteousness comes by the Law then Christ is dead in vain."** Why did God send us Jesus if we could obtain our own righteousness? **Romans 6:14** states, **"For sin shall not have dominion over you, for you are not under Law, but under grace."** And **Romans 10:4** says, **"For Christ is the end of the Law for righteousness to everyone who believes."**

If you are wondering how you can receive this gift of Eternal Life then here is a brief explanation. You must admit that you were born a sinner because of the Fall of Man. Remember **Romans 3:23** where it stated that **"all have sinned and come short of the Glory of God"**? No human being is exempt from that word *"all."* You should repent from your sins by asking God to forgive you and turn away from any form of sin by asking for Holy Spirit conviction if you do sin. Ask God to change your heart so that you can live according to His will in your life. You must believe that Jesus is the Son of God Who was sent to reverse the effects of the Fall of Man which were death and an eternal separation from God. **John 3:16** says, **"For God so loved the world that He gave His Only begotten Son, that whosoever believes on Him shall not perish but have Everlasting Life."** I am afraid that it is not just believing that Jesus *exists*, but it's believing that His death on the Cross took away your sins. **James 2:19** says, **"The Devils also believe, and tremble."** Satan believes in Jesus' existence, but the Bible is clear that he will spend eternity in the **"Lake of Fire (Revelation 21:10.)"** And finally, **Romans 9:10** states, **"If you shall confess with your mouth the Lord Jesus, and shall believe in your heart that God has raised Him from the dead, you shall be saved."** It is not something that you can intellectualize but by faith you must accept God's plan of salvation through Jesus' death on the Cross. If you are waiting until you "understand" all of this to accept it, then you may miss the opportunity.

What happens when a person becomes **"born again"** of the Spirit? Something miraculous takes place when a person accepts Jesus as Saviour. **2 Corinthians 5:17** states, **"Therefore if any man be in Christ, he is a new creature: old things are passed away; behold all things become new."** The old sin nature we were born with because of the Fall of Man is traded for a whole new life! This is only possible when we die to ourselves and allow God to transform our lives through the power of the Holy Spirit. The Sprit of God will guide you if you will keep your faith in the finished work of Jesus on the Cross. This is where Satan, sin and death were defeated once and for all. The Bible says of Jesus, **"Blotting out the handwriting of ordinances that was against us, which was contrary to us, and took it out the way, nailing it to His Cross, and having spoiled principalities and powers, He made a show of them openly, triumphing over them in it (2 Corinthians 2:14-15)."** No one will be excused when Judgment Day comes. **Romans 1:20** says, **"For the invisible things of Him from the creation of the world are clearly seen, being understood by the things that are made, even His Eternal Power and Godhead; so that they are without excuse."**

Chapter Two

AMONG THE WHEAT OR AMONG THE TARES?

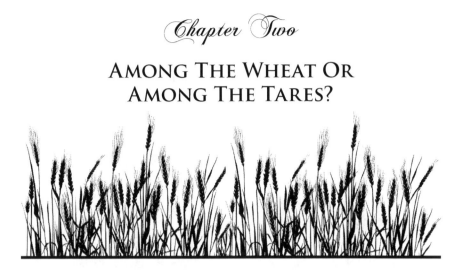

In **Matthew 13:24-30**, Jesus speaks a parable of the wheat and the tares. The Scripture states, **"Another parable put He forth unto them, saying, The Kingdom of Heaven is likened unto a Man which sowed good seed in the field. But** *while men slept,* **His enemy came and sowed tares among the wheat, and went his way. But when the blade was sprung up, and brought forth fruit, then appeared the tares also. So the servants of the householder came and said unto him, Sir, did not you sow good seed in your field? From whence then has it tares? He said unto them,** *An enemy has done this.* **The servants said unto him, Will you then that we go and gather them up? But He said, No; lest while you gather the tares, ye root up also the wheat with them. Let both grow together until the harvest: and in the time of the harvest I will say to the reapers, Gather ye together first the tares, and bind them in bundles to burn them: but gather the wheat into my barn** (my italics).**"**

Then in **Matthew 13:36-43**, Jesus explains the parable of the wheat and the tares to His Disciples leaving no room for wrong interpretation. The Scripture says, **"Then Jesus sent the multitude away, and went into the house: And His Disciples came unto Him, saying, Declare unto us the parable of the tares of the field. He answered and said unto them, He who sows the good seed is the Son of Man; The field**

is the world; the good seed are the children of the Kingdom; but the tares are children of the wicked one; The enemy that sowed them is the devil; the harvest is the end of the world; and the reapers are the Angels. As therefore the tares are gathered and burned in the fire; so shall it be in the end of this world. The Son of Man shall send forth His Angels, and they shall gather out of His Kingdom all things that offend, and them which do iniquity; And shall cast them into a furnace of fire: there shall be wailing and gnashing of teeth. Then shall the righteous shine forth as the sun in the Kingdom of their Father. Who has ears to hear, let him hear."

The variety of weed Jesus refers to as "tares" is also called "darnel" or "false wheat." It is called false wheat because as it grows it looks almost identical to true wheat. When it comes close to harvest time, the wheat turns golden brown; but the darnel turns black and is actually full of poison! The farmers in the modern wheat belt of America have to take measures to control the effects of tares on their cattle. In a 30 year study, 250,000 sheep and 600 cattle died because of it, not to mention the effects of intoxication on a score of others.[1] The symptoms concerning the consumption of darnel are: sleepiness, drowsiness, hypnotic episodes, convulsions, drunkenness, intoxication, trembling, inability to walk, hindered speech, vomiting, stupefaction, dim-sightedness. Other sites I visited include giddiness, apathy and various abnormal sensations as effects of darnel.

These symptoms describe perfectly the modern day Church world! Churches today are full of apathetic, sleeping, dim sighted "Christians," who no longer share the Gospel message of Jesus Christ and Him crucified, but are more interested in self-help or expanding the numbers in the Church pews. It is disheartening and sickening to those of us who see this damnable trend. Charles Spurgeon said, "Have you no wish for others to be saved? Then you're not saved yourself, be sure of that!"

The result of the watered down social gospel preached by many in the pulpit today is a Church full of people who are living alongside the world without any conviction of sin. One effect of darnel mentioned

---

[1]   http://www.deceptioninthechurch.com/tares.html

above is the "inability to walk," which adequately describes the sinner who has no idea how to walk in the Spirit by following the Holy Spirit's guidance. Jesus sent the Holy Spirit after His ascension into Heaven and promised that the Holy Spirit would lead us in all truth (**John 16:13**). He also guaranteed that the Holy Spirit would be our power source against the bondage of sin. He *commanded* His Disciples to wait for the Promise of the Father (**Acts 1:4**)! The majority of the Churches today do not welcome the Holy Spirit and do not encourage their believers to be baptized in the Holy Spirit with the evidence of speaking in other tongues. This phenomenal experience was recorded in **Acts 2:4**, and while many preachers today claim it was only for the early Church, I can assure you that it is not! I personally experienced it and I can tell you that it is a Gift of God that has made all of the difference in my walk with the Lord!

Before harvesting the wheat, there is time to distinguish between the darnel and the true wheat. The fruit of the darnel is smaller than the fruit produced by the wheat. Metaphorically, the fruit of the darnel is smaller represents the fact that the preachers who are teaching self-help instead of the Gospel will produce little to no fruit or "souls" for the Kingdom. The numbers in the Church pews may grow and most of these "seeker sensitive" Churches are large in number, but unfortunately, they are full of unsaved people who come to hear motivational messages each week. These messages build up the individual when in actuality, we should decrease so that the Spirit of God can increase (**John 3:30**)! Sometimes it is hard to differentiate between true or false preachers but that is why we need Holy Spirit discernment to show us more clearly who is preaching truth and who is preaching false doctrine. One earmark of a Church preaching false doctrine is that the sermons are not about Jesus and what He did on the Cross for us and about denying self by walking in the Spirit, but the sermons are all about "yourself." These "CEO pastors" deal with relationships and use bits of Scripture to give motivational pep talks to the congregation. Their Churches focus on "sermon series" which sometimes are titled after worldly Hollywood movies. Sadly, instead of seeking the Holy Spirit for a word for the people each week, many of these so called pastors get their sermon series off of paid websites and books other than the Bible. There is one thing for sure though, the One who planted the good seed which bears fruit will come back to harvest His wheat and not one grain of tare will be found in the harvest!

So, the question remains . . . *who are the wheat and who are the tares?* Remember, Jesus states in **Matthew 13:38-39** that the wheat are "**the children of the Kingdom**," which were sown by the "**Son of Man.**" However, He says that the tares are "**children of the wicked one**" and that "**the enemy that sowed them is the devil.**" The devil has sown these tares which have corrupted the true Church of Jesus Christ by introducing false doctrine, deceptive Church movements and by taking people away from the Cross, which is where Jesus paid our sin debt and bought our victory over Satan. Jesus is our only hope in glory! If you take Him out of the equation, then the result is a life of bondage to Satan and an eternity in the Lake of Fire!

Some "preachers" are intentionally preaching deceptive lies. They come in speaking truth and then introduce the leaven when they have won the hearts of the people. **Galatians 5:9** and **1 Corinthians 5:6** state, "**A little leaven leaveneth the whole lump.**" Leaven in the Bible spoke of sin and corruption. Used literally, it was a type of yeast used to make bread dough rise. Many of the Jewish feasts required unleavened bread and every speck of leaven was commanded to be expelled from the house during the preparation for these feasts because even if a little bit of leaven would get into the dough, it would eventually corrupt it and causes the dough to rise. This is the same with doctrine and just a little bit of false doctrine will corrupt the entire person over a period of time. Think of it this way, if you continually ingested a small amount of arsenic every single day, then it would eventually cause death to the body. God has called us to submit to the Holy Spirit and He will lead us into all truth and guard us against false doctrine!

Jesus also speaks in **Matthew 13:33** and **Luke 13:31** about a woman who hides leaven in three measures of meal. The Scripture in Matthew reads, "**Another parable spake he unto them; The Kingdom of Heaven is like unto leaven, which a woman took, and hid in three measures of meal, till the whole was leavened.**" This is quite an interesting parable! Frequently in Scripture, the "**woman**" is presented as an agent of idolatry. The "**meal**" is the Word of God represented here and of course, the "**leaven**" is a symbol of sin or corruption. It again shows how just a small amount of leaven can affect the entire whole. I believe you can take it even further and figure out exactly who the "**woman**" could be. The **"woman"** again shows up in the 17th Chapter of the Book of Revelation as a **"harlot"** who has corrupted the entire world with drunkenness, much like the affect the darnel has on the body. The Bible speaks of a woman, called **"the great whore"** who rides on the back of the beast, which is Antichrist **(Revelation 17:3)**. **Revelation 17:4-6** describes the woman where it says, **"And the woman was arrayed in purple and scarlet colour, and decked with gold and precious stones and pearls, having a golden cup in her hand full of abominations and filthiness of her fornication. And upon her forehead was a name written, MYSTERY, BABYLON THE GREAT, THE MOTHER OF HARLOTS AND ABOMINATIONS OF THE EARTH. And I saw the woman drunken with the blood of the Saints, and with the blood of the martyrs of Jesus . . ."** There is only one system who this Scripture describes perfectly and that is the Roman Catholic Church. She *is* **"MYSTERY BABYLON"** and **"THE MOTHER OF HARLOTS."** This Church has acquired insurmountable wealth and martyred millions of non-Catholics over the centuries. Roman Catholicism actually derived from the original Babylon in the Book of Genesis where idolatry was first introduced. After Noah's flood, Satan used Nimrod to build a city called Babylon and to construct a tower which would attempt to reach Heaven **(Genesis 11:4)**. Nimrod, his mother and then his wife, Semiramis, began the practice of astrology and of child sacrifice in Babylon. It is believed that Noah's son, Shem, killed Nimrod to end these occult practices. Once Nimrod was dead, Semiramis quickly made him into a god and demanded that he be worshipped. She then became pregnant and claimed that it was through a virgin conception. She gave birth to a son who she named Tammuz. Semiramis convinced the people that she had given birth to the reincarnated Nimrod and that he was the "savior" of the people. Semiramis soon became the moon god and was also called the "Queen of Heaven." Statues of her appeared holding a baby boy, which she claimed to be the savior. Nimrod or "Baal" became the sun god.[2] The people worshipped the sun because it was thought to bring life. They also worshipped the male reproductive organ because of the fact that it too was instrumental in the creation of life. This is the beginnings of sun and moon worship and the fertility cults which are still alive and well today.

---

[2]   *The Two Babylons*, Alexander Hislop, Loizeaux Brothers, 1959, page 43

All of the ancient mystery religions came from the Tower of Babel because when God confounded the languages and dispersed the people, they carried these pagan practices with them. The religion of Nimrod and Semiramis spread into Egypt as well. Soon sun and moon worship became the religion of the land. The sun god became known as Osiris and the moon god as Isis in the powerful Egyptian region. These two gods became known by different names in different cultures but they all can be traced back to Babylon.

The offspring of Isis and Osiris was known as Horus, the divine child, and collectively they were known as the Egyptian trinity. This is where the fertility cults originated with the sun representing the male deity and the moon as the female deity. The Egyptian priests claimed to have magical powers which enabled them to change a circular wafer of bread, shaped like the sun, into the god of Osiris. The religious faithful would eat this unleavened bread to "nourish their souls," just as the ancient Babylonian priests of Nimrod's day.[3] In the Bible, Egypt represented "the world" and the powerful Pharaohs represented "Satan."

Let us compare the pagan Babylonian and Egyptian practices to the practices of the Roman Catholic Church. The Roman Catholic "Jesus" is a wafer of bread shaped like a circle, much like what the ancient Babylonians and Egyptians ate to "nourish their souls." The Roman Catholic Eucharist taken at Mass is believed to be *the literal body of Jesus Christ*. They teach that Jesus offers Himself as the victim when the "host" or wafer is consecrated at each and every Mass. "Hostia" in Latin means "victim." They further believe that when the priest magically consecrates the wafer, it changes it into the *true body and divinity* of Jesus Christ, as the wine is turned into the *true blood* of Jesus. Roman Catholic Canon Law states, "If any one shall deny that the body and blood, together with the souls an divinity of our Lord Jesus Christ, and therefore entire Christ, are truly, really, and substantially contained in the sacrament of the most Holy Eucharist; and shall say that He is only in it as a sign, or in a figure, let him be accursed."[4] Accursed means to be damned to Hell for all of eternity.

---

[3] *The Two Babylons*, Alexander Hislop, Loizeaux Brothers, 1959, page 20,160-161,164

[4] Roman Catholic Code of Canon Law *Council of Trent* Canon I

In the Book of Jeremiah, Egypt's conquest by the Babylonian Empire is foretold (**Jeremiah 46:13-26**) and then in the Book of Daniel, we see the Roman Empire take control of Egypt (**Daniel 11:14**). We will dig into the Book of Daniel very soon where the power shifts of the great empires of the world were predicted. It is most interesting to see the future foretold in God's Word and then to read how and when it was fulfilled!

Many prophecy scholars claim that **"the woman"** or **"whore"** of **Revelation 17** is the one world religious system under the false prophet and the Antichrist which is yet to come. I do agree with this statement and do not think that it contradicts the fact that I believe that she is the Church of Rome. There *will be* an end time one world religion and I believe that the pope of Rome and the Roman Catholic Church will be the key in this scenario. Why do I believe this? Because the preparation for the New World Order religion has been paved by the Ecumenical Movement which was spearheaded by Pope John Paul II, continued to gain acceptance under Pope Benedict XVI and now is being promoted even more feverishly by Pope Francis I.

Pope Benedict XVI issued an encyclical before he left the papal office called, *"Caritas in Veritate* (Charity in Truth)." In this encyclical, the pope explained that a "World Political Authority" was necessary in order to "manage the global economy; to revive economies hit by the crisis; to avoid any deterioration of the present crisis and the greater imbalances that would result; to bring about integral and timely disarmament, food security and peace; to guarantee the protection of the environment and to regulate migration . . ."

The proposed New World Order cannot stand without a global religion. Christopher Dawson, a Roman Catholic historian wrote, "It is the religious impulse which supplies the cohesive force which unifies a society and a culture. The great civilizations of the world do not produce the great religions as a kind of cultural byproduct; in a very real sense, the great religions are the foundations on which the great civilizations rest."[5] Lally Lucretia Warren, a leader of the 2004 Parliament of World

---

[5]   *Progress and Religion,* Christopher Dawson, Image Books, 1960, page 18

Religions from Botswana, also stated, "Religion is the chief instrument through which order is established in the world."[6] The bottom line is that *religion* is the basis for an enduring civilization.

The religious system taking shape right now very likely will incorporate all of the major religions into one system of theology without actually changing the individual basic belief systems. It will basically be a world system of *religious tolerance*. As lovely as this "religion of tolerance" sounds, it is completely contrary to what the Bible teaches regarding salvation.

Many want to believe that "there are many paths to Heaven," but in **Matthew 7:13-14** Jesus says, **"Enter you in at the strait gate: for wide *is* the gate, and broad is the way, that leads to destruction, and many there be which go in thereat: Because strait *is* the gate, and narrow *is* the way, which leads unto life, and few there be that find it."** The many different paths to Heaven are the **"wide"** and **"broad"** gate which Jesus speaks of, and He specifically says that this way **"leads to destruction."** However, He says that those who take the **"strait"** and **"narrow"** gate, it **"leads unto life,"** meaning Eternal Life. This explanation could not be any clearer. Only *one* of these gates leads to Heaven and there are few who find it according to the Scripture. It may not appear to be the most attractive gate because it discourages the carnal pleasures of the world. The narrow gate may be difficult to even look upon because it makes a person feel conviction for living in sin. It is certainly not widely accepted, but it is still the *only* way. Jesus said in **John 14:6**, **". . . I am the Way, the Truth, and the Life: no man comes unto the Father, but by me."** Jesus is the only way to the Father which is in Heaven, where we all strive to go when we leave this Earth. In **John 10:1**, Jesus says, **"Verily, Verily, I say unto you, He who enters by the door into the sheepfold, but climbs up some other way, the same is a thief and a robber. But he who enters in by the Door** (Jesus is the Door—**John 10:7**) **is the Shepherd of the sheep."** Then **Acts 4:12** says, **"Neither is there Salvation in any other for there is none other Name**

---

6   *Jewish World Review*, Geneive Abdo, "Can a parliament of leaders from traditional religions and those with a more New Age flavor save the world from itself?", July 8, 2004

under Heaven given among men, whereby we must be saved." Jesus is the only *Name, Way, Door or Gate* by which we will see Heaven!

In describing the **"woman"** who hid the leaven in the meal and corrupted the whole, the question may arise: Am I insinuating that the Roman Catholic religion is "leaven?" Would you believe that the Roman Catholic Church believes and even *boasts* that they are leaven in the world? *The Catechism of the Catholic Church* states, "The characteristics of a lay state being a life led in the midst of the world and in secular affairs, lay people are called of God to make of their apostolate, through the vigor of their Christian spirit, a leaven in the world (940)." Here is more from the same source, "By a life perfectly and entirely consecrated to such sanctification, the members of these institutes share in the Churches task of evangelization, 'in the world and from within the world' where their presence acts as 'leaven in the world (929).'" Pope John Paul II called for the faithful members of the Roman Catholic Church to *"Be a Gospel Leaven in Society."* He said, "I give my encouragement and support to the lay faithful of this blessed land of Georgia. In your families, your parishes and in your associations, celebrate your faith in Christ and be a leaven of the Gospel in society around you . . ." Pope Francis I addressed the people of Rio de Janeiro on July 27, 2013 by saying, "Peaceful coexistence between different religions is favored by the laicity of the state which . . . respects and esteems the presence of the religious factor in society, while fostering its concrete expressions." He also said that the great religious traditions "play a fruitful role as leaven of society, and a life giving force for democracy."[7]

The Bible says in **Isaiah 5:20, "Woe unto them who call evil good, and good evil . . ."** This is exactly what is happening here! "Leaven" in the Bible obviously has a negative connotation, so why would *The Catechism of the Catholic Church* and two popes of the Roman Catholic Church encourage their faithful followers to be "leaven" in society?

Let us rewind a bit where Jesus is warning what will happen to the tares at harvest time. **"The servants said unto him, Will you then that we go and gather them up? But He said, No; lest while you gather the**

---

[7]   http://www.catholicnewsagency.com/news/religion-is-leaven-in-society-pope-tells-brazils-leaders/

tares, ye root up also the wheat with them. Let both grow together until the harvest: and in the time of the harvest I will say to the reapers, Gather ye together first the tares, and bind them in bundles to burn them: but gather the wheat into my barn (Matthew 13:28-30)." In **Jeremiah 51** and in **Revelation 14 and 18** we see Babylon, which represents false religion, burned by fire until it is destroyed. And in Matthew Chapter 13, Jesus is saying that the wheat and tares will be separated and the tares will be bound and burned. This is nothing to be taken lightly; I shed tears as I write this. The world along with the majority of the Christian world has been deceived and will fall into the category of "tares" at harvest time. The next chapter will show how the Church world fits into this deception through the many Church movements which have swept Jesus Christ and His finished work on the Cross under the rug, trading Him for pleasure and acceptance to the world system. Matthew's Gospel clearly says that *"while men slept . . ."* this deception took place. Let me end this chapter with a question posed to the reader: Where will Jesus find you at harvest time: among the wheat or among the tares?

Chapter Three

CONSPIRACY THEORY OR JUST THE FACTS?

Do you find yourself wondering if all of the bizarre events going on in the world today are mere coincidences or pieces of a bigger picture purposefully orchestrated? If you are anything like me, you have serious suspicions that things are not quite as they seem. Eight years ago, I did something that completely changed my life: I accepted Jesus Christ as the Lord of my life and the Saviour of my soul. If that was not exciting enough, a year later I was baptized in the Holy Spirit with the evidence of speaking in other tongues. It was a short six months later when I began writing my first book to my family explaining God's redemption plan through Jesus' sacrifice which is found in the Bible. As I researched, I learned a great deal about other religions, mostly Roman Catholicism, and also looked deeply into some of these new Church movements which seemed to be taking people away from redemption through the death of Jesus on the Cross but were more geared toward humanism and psychology.

In researching, I began to see many connections which kept me digging deeper and deeper. As I would seek the Lord and He would reveal more to me, the puzzle pieces began to fit into place and the picture created was almost unbelievable! I suppose that I am curious by nature and I was determined to figure out if there was a common denominator which was pushing the plan of Satan forward. I began to realize that Satan uses many techniques to confuse and deceive mankind into going his way instead of God's way. *Religion* is certainly one of his most successful tools mainly because the doing of religion appeals to man's flesh and makes him *feel good*; it is often called an "opiate." Unfortunately, religion only creates a self-righteous spirit as opposed to a humble and contrite spirit which is produced when self is denied and a person's life is submitted to God's will through the leading of the Holy Spirit as the Bible teaches.

There is a great deal of Scripture in the Bible warning about false doctrine, false teachers and false prophets. Why would God put so much emphasis on this particular subject? Because He is omniscient, He knew that false doctrine would eventually plague the Church. In the Bible, it did not take long from the time when the Apostles and Disciples were shouting, **"But we preach Christ Crucified" (1 Corinthians 1:23)** and setting up Churches in the Book of Acts, before the Churches began teaching error. Most of Paul's Epistles to the Churches were corrections to those congregations heading away from the Cross and back to the Law. Sadly, this was just 20 to 25 years after Jesus had ascended into Heaven!

Today we have Humanistic Psychology plaguing the Church which was made popular by Sigmund Freud, an atheist and cocaine user.[8] He often prescribed cocaine to his patients in an attempt to improve their mental health.[9] Humanistic Psychology denies a soul and a spirit, which is contrary to the Biblical teaching that God created us with both. The father of Analytical Psychology, Carl Jung, was led by a demon spirit guide named Philemon.[10] These are the men who are responsible for the modern psychology used today; an atheist and a man led by a demon spirit! This easily verifies that *psychology is not of God*, so the fact that it is rampant in many Churches today is heartbreaking!

We also have the New Age movement or the "New Spirituality" which began in the early 1900's and was introduced by a Roman Catholic Jesuit priest named Pierre Teilhard de Chardin. This theology has spread like wildfire into health care, education and Christianity. Then

---

[8]   http://www.pbs.org/wgbh/questionofgod/twolives/freudbio.html
[9]   http://www.freudfile.org/cocaine.html
[10]   http://www.philipcoppens.com/jung.html

the "Seeker Sensitive" Church movement began with men such as Rick Warren and Bill Hybels who wanted to create Churches where the people of the congregation decided what type of music should be played and what style of preaching they would like to hear. Do you think that people wanted to hear that they were born sinners and had to accept an innocent Man's death on the Cross to be saved? Of course not! Basically their congregations get motivational pep talks each week at Church. Some Churches even serve refreshments and have coffee shops inside of the Church! The music of the world is often brought into these Churches sometimes using darkened rooms and disco lights as you would see in a night club venue. It is hardly an atmosphere for the Holy Spirit to dwell. However, demons spirits gladly thrive in it!

Rick Warren then became extremely popular when his books, *The Purpose Driven Church* and *The Purpose Driven Life* became bestsellers. Rick Warren has introduced his "40 Days of Purpose" and "40 Days of Community" into hundreds of thousands of Churches all over the world. This is what Rick Warren had to say about his "40 days of Community" program, "The Tower of Babel was a perfect example of what could be accomplished when men and women work together to reach a common goal." Remember that the Godhead was so displeased with the creation of the Tower of Babel that they destroyed the plans of the men who were building it! *Please take a close look at Rick Warren* and what he has done to the true Church of Jesus Christ. His Purpose Driven program has infected hundreds of thousands of Churches around the world causing them to water down the Word of God and preach a social feel-good gospel. You will soon see that this was the direct plan of those trying to infiltrate America and deceive the nation into joining a unified one world government in the late 1800's and early 1900's. This would be the same one world government mentioned in the Bible which Antichrist will control. I would say that Rick Warren has accomplished his success single-handedly, but I suspect that he has had some help along the way. Businessman Peter Drucker was Warren's mentor for many years until Drucker died in 2005. Warren stated, ". . . Now Drucker has said that at least six times. I happen to know because he's *my mentor.* I've spent 20 years under his tutelage learning about leadership from him, and he's written it in two or three books, and he says he thinks it's [the mega-church] the only thing that really works in society."[11]

Drucker envisioned the collaboration of the public sector of the government, the private sector of the business world and the social sector of the Church as a "three legged stool."[12] He believed that the only way to achieve order was to combine these three separate sectors.[13] Peter Drucker also greatly admired Ignatius Loyola's move to create the Roman Catholic Jesuit Order and referred to them as, "the most successful staff organization in the world."[14] Not only has Drucker been a mentor for Rick Warren, but he also helped him to establish "Purpose-Driven" as a major name brand in the evangelical market. Peter Drucker once said of Rick Warren, "Warren is not building a tent revival ministry, like the old-style evangelists. He's building an army, like the Jesuits."[15]

The most recent Church movement would be the Emerging Church movement which is an extension of the Seeker Sensitive and Purpose Driven Church movements. The Emerging Church was also endorsed by Peter Drucker under an organization called "Leadership Network," which eventually became known as "The Emergent Church." Not only does this movement promote religious tolerance, but they also incorporate a lot of New Age concepts such as contemplative prayer, a form of transcendental meditation, where the person is encouraged to empty their minds in order to fall into an altered state of consciousness. This is the same as Ignatius Loyola's *Spiritual Exercises* used by the Jesuit superiors to get the Jesuit initiates completely under their control! You will see the significance and power of the Jesuit Order as you continue to read this book. The Emerging Churches, with leaders such as Brian McLaren, Doug Pagitt and Dan Kimball encourage their congregations to participate in very Roman Catholic traditions such as Advent, Lent, Stations of the Cross and more. When you dig deeper into all of these Church movements, you begin to see the same common denominator every time! The words

---

[11] http://pewforum.org/events/index.php?EventID=80
[12] http://www.discernment-ministries.org/ChristianImperialism.htm
[13] http://www.discernment-ministries.org/ChristianImperialism.htm
[14] http://www.accessmylibrary.com/article-1G1-142591811/jesuit-priests-invented-feedback.html
[15] *New Yorker Magazine,* "The Cellular Church," by Malcolm Gladwell, 9/12/05

"Roman Catholic" and "Jesuit Order" keep showing up as the facilitators. There is a popular phrase that states, "All roads lead to Rome . . ." Well, you can believe it! Here is some proof of how Rome is responsible for the apathetic state of the Church today.

After WWII, too many people were aware that the Vatican was responsible for the war and so Roman Catholicism as a whole needed to change its public image. In 1962, the *Vatican II Council* convened and the Roman Catholic Church suddenly appeared to change its hatred toward the Protestants and non-Catholics, whom they had been killing in their awful inquisitions for centuries. Instead of calling them "heretics," as they had been all down the centuries, they referred to them as "separated brethren."[16] Rome even began to call Catholics by the name of "Christians," which was a clever idea confusing the generations which were to follow. Before this time, the Catholics and Christians were two separated groups.[17] It only takes approximately two generations for everything to be forgotten and the Roman Catholic Church has attempted to rewrite history to cover up their wicked past.

The *Vatican II Council* of 1962 ushered in an "Ecumenical Movement" which would deceive billions of people. The 1960's became the era of "peace," but if you will think about it, it was also the "hippie" era where sex, drugs and rock and roll were at their height. It is interesting to note that international drug trafficking is orchestrated by the Jesuit General through the CIA and the Mafia. He uses the proceeds to finance his international terrorist network. All of the terrorist networks work together; Hamas, PLO, and Al-Qaeda just to name a few.[18]

Then in 1986, Pope John Paul II invited 160 religious leaders from 12 major religions of the world to St. Peter's Basilica for prayer where the pope claimed that they were all praying to the same god.[19] This was a time where the **"MOTHER OF HARLOTS" (Revelation 17:5)** invited many of her "daughters" back into the fold. Not long after, in 1994, the Roman Catholics and many influential evangelical leaders signed a joint

[16] *Smokescreens*, Jack Chick, Chick Publications, 1983, page 45
[17] *The Final Apostasy Unveiled*, Kevin Hall, Derek Press, 2006, pages 48-49
[18] *Vatican Assassins*, Eric Jon Phelps, pages 564,566,587,630
[19] http://en.wikipedia.org/wiki/_John_Paul_II

declaration entitled: "Evangelicals and Catholics Together: The Christian Mission in the Third Millennium."[20] The question must be asked, "Has the Roman Catholic Church *truly* changed?

It seems that before the inquisitions and massacres where millions of Protestant "heretics," among others, were tortured and killed, the Roman Catholic Church befriended them and made them feel as if they could let their guards down for a while and live peaceably together. Then when the pope would give the signal, the Roman Catholic priests and faithful members would suddenly turn on the Protestants and massacre them by the thousands.[21] They tortured the Protestants in the most ungodly fashions and then killed them, as well as, any Roman Catholics who were sympathetic to the Protestants. Could this time of "peace" which began in 1962 actually be a front to deceive the true Christians and non-Catholics into letting their guards down, all the while they are preparing for a new inquisition; the one which is described in the Book of Revelation? Does Rome still have the power to accomplish this feat? Many claim and believe she doesn't but let us look at the Book of Daniel which will clarify when exactly that Rome became the controlling power of the world and also to see if there has been a period in history when the Roman Empire was defeated.

---

[20] *A Woman Rides the Beast,* Dave Hunt, Harvest House Publishers, Oregon, 1994, page 5

[21] *Smokescreens,* Jack Chick, Chick Publications, 1983, page 17

Chapter Four

HISTORY FORETOLD . . . THE BOOK OF DANIEL

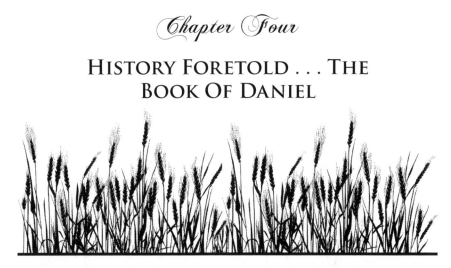

The book of Daniel has been referred to as the "Revelation of the Old Testament." It presents Daniel's visions revealing God's plan and purposes in the unfolding of future events. Daniel was shown the future of nations and empires all of the way through to the second coming of Jesus Christ. The great prophet pinpointed the rise of the Antichrist, the location of his empire, as well as, so many of the particulars leading up to the second coming of Christ. Daniel was given remarkable insight concerning the end times which is so important for us today because we are living in the last of the last days.

Civilization started in the Euphrates valley and according to the Bible, it is going to end there as well. Basically, what we are seeing now is the beginning of the end. Correctly understanding Scripture demands that the pieces fit all the way from the Book of Genesis to the Book of Revelation. It is very easy to form a doctrine out of a portion of Scripture instead of looking at the entire picture. This inevitably leads to wrong interpretation and therefore, error. We need to understand that prophecy is actually history written in advance. The Bible's plain and simple statements should be taking literally whenever it is possible. If symbolism is used, we must try to understand the message behind the symbolism. For example, when the Lord said, **"you are the salt of the earth,"** He did not mean that the child of God is made up of the compound sodium chloride. He simply meant that salt is a preservative which adds flavor and can keep food from spoiling, which the child of God, likewise, preserves a system that would otherwise self-destruct. The whole Bible is made up of about one third prophecy and there are over 300 prophecies in the Old Testament concerning the coming of the Messiah. These were all fulfilled in Jesus Christ who became man to save those who would believe in the sacrificial offering of Himself on the Cross.

Daniel was born in Israel, around the year of 615 B.C. He died in the province of Babylon; it is thought in 534 B.C. in the third year of Cyrus, King of Persia. He was likely around 80 years of age at the time of his death. Daniel was a contemporary of Jeremiah and Ezekiel, who prophesied the captivity of Israel, which Daniel actually witnessed firsthand. Jesus referred to Daniel as a prophet and even quoted him in **Matthew 24:15**. Daniel was forced into exile in 605 B.C. and he was among the first group carried captive into Babylon. It was during the reign of Jehoiakim, King of Judah, that Nebuchadnezzar came from Babylon and captured this group of individuals. Daniel was taken captive when he was approximately 10 or 11 years old.

The unique story of the Book of Daniel is that it predicted, almost to the day, the crucifixion of the Messiah **(Daniel 9:25-26)**. Therefore, Israel was without excuse with its condemnation of Jesus as an imposter. Had not this prophecy been given to Daniel, the nation would not have known when the Redeemer was to appear.

God made Israel the center of a system of nations, people, and languages that arose in consequence of the judgment on Babel and had committed the scepter of world power to her hand **(Deuteronomy 32:8)**. But as a consequence of her persistent idolatry, He took that scepter from her and placed it in the hands of Nebuchadnezzar and his successors, where it remains still to this present day. The Book of Daniel occupies itself with the rise and fall of successive governments, and with a remnant of Israel in subjection to them, and it closes with the substitution of the Kingdom of the Messiah, which is yet to be established upon the Earth. The prophecies of this book cover the period of human history referred to as **"the times of the Gentiles (Luke 21:24)."** It reaches from Nebuchadnezzar's reign until the destruction of the Antichrist and his system.

In **Daniel 2:31-34**, Daniel interprets Nebuchadnezzar's dream. The description reads, "**You, O King, saw, and behold a great image. This great image, whose brightness was excellent, stood before you; and the form thereof was terrible. This images head was a fine gold, his breast and his arms of silver, his belly and his thighs of brass, his legs of iron, his feet part of iron and part of clay. You saw till that a stone was cut out without hands, which smote the image upon his feet that were of iron and clay, and broke them into pieces.**"

He explains the meaning of the statue to King Nebuchadnezzar in **Daniel 2: 36-44** where the Scripture says, "**This is the dream; and we will tell the interpretation there of before the king. You, O King, are a king of kings: for the God of heaven has given you a kingdom, power, and strength, and glory. And after you shall arise another kingdom inferior to you, and another third kingdom of brass, which shall bear rule over all the Earth. And the fourth kingdom shall be strong as iron: forasmuch as iron breaks in pieces and subdues all things: and as iron that breaks all things shall it break in pieces and bruise. And whereas you saw the feet and toes, part of Potters Clay, and part of iron, the kingdom shall be divided; but there shall be in it of the strength of the iron, forasmuch as you saw the iron mixed with the miry clay. And as the toes of the feet were part of iron, and part of clay, so the kingdom shall be partly strong, and partly broken. And whereas you saw iron mixed with miry clay, they shall mingle themselves with the seed of men: but they shall not cleave one to another, even as iron is not mixed with clay. And in the days of these kings shall the God of Heaven set up a kingdom, which shall never be destroyed: in the kingdom shall not be left to other people, but it shall break in pieces and consume all these kingdoms, and it shall stand forever.**"

"**This head of gold**" represented the Babylonian Empire. The phrase, "**and after you shall arise another kingdom inferior to you,**" referred to the inferiority only in the capacity of wealth and grandness. This was the Medo-Persian Empire represented by **"two arms"** of the image making the dual kingdom. This empire lasted for a period of over 200 years, from about 540-332 B.C. The phrase, **"and another third kingdom of brass, which shall bear rule over all the earth,"** represented the Grecian Empire, which followed Medo-Persia. It is represented by the **"belly and thighs of brass"** on the image and it lasted from 332-186 B.C. but began to crumble and decay after the death of Alexander the Great at the age of 32. His vast territory was divided into four parts after his death. The fourth kingdom mentioned as the **"legs of iron"** represented the Roman Empire. The two legs represented the Eastern and Western division which were split in the "Great Schism" of 1054. The Roman Empire was in power when Jesus was born. The phrase, **"And the fourth Kingdom shall be strong as iron,"** represents the Roman Empire as the strongest of them all! The phrase, **"Forasmuch as iron breaks into pieces and subdues all things: and as iron that breaks all these, shall it break in pieces and bruise,"** refers to the ruthless nature of the Roman Empire.

The Old Roman Empire was ruled by one man, the Caesar, as Rome was involved in Emperor Worship. The four empires given in **Daniel 2:36-45** were: the Babylonian, the Medo-Persian, the Greek and the Roman. It was Rome that was in power at the time of Jesus' birth on Earth and after His death, resurrection and ascension; it was Rome who continued to persecute the early Church under the leadership of the Apostles and Disciples of Jesus who were called to preach the Gospel to the world. Rome has never ceased to be a political empire but was only split into the East and West divisions after Constantine. Around the year 313 A.D., a Roman Emperor named Constantine issued the Edict of Milan. This letter gave Christians the opportunity to worship as they desired without fear of persecution within the Roman Empire. Some Christians of the early Church, tired of persecution, accepted this offer and this acceptance is what meshed the pagan Roman practice of Emperor Worship with true Christianity. The result became the apostate Church of Roman Catholicism. Because Christianity was recognized alongside the old paganism, Constantine set himself up as the leader of this new Church. Constantine married the Church and the state and called himself the "vicar of Christ," which is still the official title of the pope of the Roman Catholic Church to this very day. This new mesh of Christianity and pagan Roman traditions combined to form a universal Church which was named the "Catholic Church," because the word "catholic" actually means "universal." Of course, there was a remnant that did not join with this new "universal" Church, as God always has a remnant that does not depart from His Word.

An interesting point is that if this Church was only a "universal" Church which was welcome to all, then why did it evolve into the *Roman* Catholic Church? It is specifically tied to the oppressive Roman system which was in place during the time of Jesus' first coming and has only continued to attempt to rule the world of today! The Roman Catholic Church, under the leadership of the pope, claims to have *Universal Spiritual Power*, which was issued by Pope Phocus in 606 A.D. and *Universal Temporal Power*, where the pope has the right to rule *every government* of the world including *every person* on the face of the Earth, by Pope Pepin in 756 A.D. These two powers are very important in understanding the papal system and the goal of the Roman Catholic Church to bring every person and every nation under her submission. The two keys on the papal crest represent these two powers. The Roman Empire has *never* been defeated. The Bible distinctly shows the overthrow of all of the other empires but Rome's defeat is never mentioned. They were in control when Jesus was born and it was the Roman General Titus who destroyed the Jewish Temple in 70 A.D.

In researching written history, outside of the Bible, one finds that there are claims that the Fall of Rome happened in 476 A.D. under various barbarians and also a German leader named Odoacer who allegedly captured Rome and set himself up as Emperor. However, it was also made known that Odoacer decided *not* to execute Romulus Augustus, who was the Roman Emperor at the time of his siege. It was also written in the same article that "The Roman Empire rebounded from a third century collapse. However, it never returned to glory. Despite this, the empire appeared to be secure and perpetual into the late fourth century. In the fifth century, events conspired against the empire. A series of crises and barbarian incursions weakened the west. Rome was sacked twice in the century. By 476, Germanic leader Odoacer decided the empire was no longer relevant and renounced the emperorship." [22] Basically, in the conclusion of the article, Rome is not seen as completely defeated, but only weakened and the German leader thought it to be so weak that it became "no longer relevant" and he renounced his emperorship. Now, let's say that this is the truth, and perhaps it is, but it still does not confirm the absolute destruction of Rome! This Empire is still alive today, still has Church and state married and comes in the form of the Roman Catholic Church under the authority of the pope!

If one could notice in the statue depicted in Nebuchadnezzar's dream, there is degeneration in value concerning the metals, but yet an increase in strength. Excluding the mixture of iron and clay, of course, and this is where the iron is weakened. I believe the mixture of the iron and clay is symbolic of the Ecumenical Movement that began partly in 1962 with the Vatican II Council and then in 1986, it was fueled by Pope John Paul II inviting 160 religious leaders from 12 major religions of the world to St. Peter's for prayer where he claimed that they were all praying to the same god.[23] And, of course, in 1994, when Roman Catholics and many prominent Evangelical leaders signed the joint declaration entitled: "Evangelicals and Catholics Together: The Christian Mission in the Third Millennium."[24] Some Evangelical leaders who signed that joint declaration were: Pat Robertson, Chuck Colson, John White, former president of the National Association of Evangelicals, and Bill Bright of Campus Crusade for Christ. Other Evangelical endorsers included the head of the Home Missions Board and Christian Life Commission of the Southern Baptist Convention, the nation's largest Protestant denomination. The president of Fuller Theological Seminary signed it, as well as two Assemblies of God preachers, who may or may not have represented the General Counsel of the Assemblies of God.[25]

Sadly, there is just a small remnant of true blood bought believers who have not adhered to this Ecumenical Movement which Rome

---

[22] http://www.examiner.com/article/the-fall-of-the-roman-empire-450-476-a-d

[23] http://en.wikipedia.org/wiki/_John_Paul_II

[24] *A Woman Rides the Beast*, Dave Hunt, Harvest House Publishers, Oregon, 1994, page 5

[25] *Bible Commentary on Daniel*, Jimmy Swaggart, World Evangelism Press, 2004, page 74

has orchestrated. We are seen as fundamentalist and even downright dangerous because we base our beliefs on God's Word alone. The Lord warned us in **2 Thessalonians 2:3-4** where Paul says, **"Let no man deceive you by any means: for that day shall not come, except there come a falling away first, and that man of sin be revealed, the son of perdition** (Antichrist). **Who opposes and exalts himself above all that is called God, or that he as God sits in the Temple of God, showing himself that he is God."** Here we see the description of the coming Antichrist who will *claim* to be God, and also we see the prophecy of the **"falling away"** which is already happening in the Churches of today.

Many Churches of every denomination are **"falling away"** from the true Gospel message of **"Jesus Christ and Him Crucified" (1 Corinthians 2:2).** They are moving into man-made disciplines and self-help programs which are not only unscriptural, but are also an abomination in the eyes of God. I truly believe that those **"who have ears to hear"** and **"who have eyes to see"** can see it just as clear as day! This book is a plea to wake up those who have fallen into this "one world religion of tolerance" trap, which the Antichrist system is quickly setting up.

The **"Stone"** cut without hands referred to in **Daniel 2:34** is the Lord Jesus Christ! Then in **Daniel 2:35** it says, **"then what the iron, the clay, and brass, the silver, and the gold, broken to pieces together, and became like the chaff of the summer threshing floors; And the wind carried them away, that no place was found for them: in the stone that smote the image became a great mountain, and filled the whole Earth."** This refers to the second coming of the Lord, when all of the nations of the world will be broken into pieces together and none will be excluded! Man's time, referred to as the **"times of the Gentiles,"** will then have ended permanently.

In Daniel Chapters 7 through 12, he deals with the successive empires but he is mainly occupied with the predictions of the **"fourth beast"** where the **"little horn"** is introduced. Any Bible scholar will agree that the **"little horn"** is the Antichrist! Daniel describes these dreams and visions in **Daniel 7:1-8** where it states, **"In the first year of Belshazzar King of Babylon Daniel had a dream and visions of his head upon his bed: then he wrote the dream, and told the sum of the** matters. Daniel spoke and said, I saw in my vision by night, and, behold, the four winds of the heaven strove upon the great sea. And four great beasts came up from the sea, diverse one from another. The first was like a lion, and had eagle's wings: I beheld till the wings thereof were plucked, and it was lifted up from the Earth, and made stand upon the feet as a man, and a man's heart was given to it. And behold another beast, a second, like to a bear, and it raised up itself on one side, and it had three ribs in the mouth of it between the teeth of it: and they said thus unto it, Arise, devour much flesh. After this I beheld, and lo another, like a leopard, which had upon the back of it four wings of a fowl; the beast had also four heads; and dominion was given to it. After this I saw in the night visions, and behold a fourth beast, dreadful and terrible, and strong exceedingly and it had great iron teeth: it devoured and broke in pieces, and stamped the residue with the feet of it; and was diverse from all the beasts that were before it; and it had ten horns. I considered the horns, and, behold, there came up among them another little horn, before whom there were three of the first horns plucked up by the roots: and, behold, in this horn were the eyes like the eyes of a man, and a mouth speaking great things."

These **"beasts"** symbolically represent kingdoms and their rulers, and more than all, the fallen angels under Satan's dominion which are behind these kingdoms. The vision and the dream were similar to the dream given to Nebuchadnezzar, which had been given by God in the form of a statue. It was represented by gold, silver, brass, iron and iron/clay mixture; however, the dreams and visions which were given to Daniel, concerning the same empires, were given in the form of **"beasts."** Why the difference? The statue that Nebuchadnezzar saw in his dream represented these great empires *as man sees them*. However the dreams and visions that God gave to Daniel, showing the empires as ferocious beasts, are *as God sees them*, and in fact, as they actually are.

These empires, which were symbolically represented by various animals, concern empires which would greatly persecute Israel. Even though the Medo-Persian Empire, which was represented by a **"bear,"** allowed the Jews to go back to Judah, it remained a vassal state, and therefore, subject to the Medo-Persian Empire. Actually, the greatest persecution of all has and will come under the **"fourth beast,"** which will produce the **"ten horns"** of the latter days, and more especially, the **"little horn,"** who is the Antichrist, and who will attempt to completely destroy Israel.

The word "horn" is symbolic of authority and power. It says in the Scripture above that **"in this horn were the eyes like the eyes of man, and a mouth speaking great things."** It states in **Daniel 8:25, "And through his policy also shall cause craft to prosper in his hand; and he shall magnify himself in his heart, and by *peace* shall destroy many: he shall also stand up against the Prince of princes; but he shall be broken without hand** (my italics)." Then in **Daniel 11:21**, it speaks of Antiochus Epiphanes, who was a forerunner to Antichrist, doing much of what it is predicted the future Antichrist will do. It says, **"And in his estate shall stand up a vile person, to whom they shall not give the honour of the kingdom: but he shall come in *peaceably, and obtain the kingdom by flatteries* (my italics)."** You will see in a future chapter how this prophecy is being fulfilled *right now*!

Daniel first speaks of a beast like a lion with eagle's wings which referred to the Babylonian Empire. Then in verse 5 he speaks of another beast, in the appearance of a bear with three ribs in its mouth between its teeth. This was symbolic of the Medo-Persian Empire and the three ribs in the mouth of the bear symbolize the conquest of Babylon, Lydia and Egypt. Then Daniel speaks of another beast like a leopard which had upon its back four wings of a fowl. The beast had four heads and dominion was given to it representing the Grecian Empire under Alexander the Great. The four heads speak of the manner in which this empire was broken into four divisions after the death of Alexander. The "dominion" refers to the four generals who took the empire after Alexander's death, dominating their respective kingdoms: Greece, Thrace, Syria and Egypt.

When Daniel gets to the description of the fourth beast, he is almost dumbfounded by its appearance! It is unlike any animal he has *ever* seen and he can only describe what he sees as **"dreadful and terrible," "strong exceedingly,"** having **"great iron teeth."** Daniel states that it **"had ten horns"** with a **"little horn"** and was diverse from all of the other beasts he had already described. He also adds a little while later in **Daniel 7:23**, **"The fourth beast shall be the fourth kingdom upon the Earth, which shall be diverse from all kingdoms, and shall devour the whole Earth, and shall tread it down and break it to pieces."** The Roman kingdom he speaks of is a monster of great proportions which subdues and devours the whole Earth! We are not talking about a kingdom which has disappeared over the centuries. Rome is alive and well, and the deception she is capable of has misled even the very elect of God!

I hate to end this chapter with the threat of the **"fourth beast"** and Daniel's warnings concerning this powerful empire. The good news is that Daniel does predict the overcoming of the Saints! In **Daniel 7: 15-18, 22** and **27** it says, **"I Daniel was grieved in my spirit in the midst of my body, and the visions of my head troubled me. I came near unto one of them who stood by** (an angel), **and asked him the truth of all this. So he told me, and made me know the interpretations of things. These great beasts, which are four, are four kings, which shall rise out of the Earth. But the Saints of the most High shall take the kingdom, and possess the kingdom forever even for ever and ever . . . Until the ancient of the days came, and judgment was given to the Saints of the Most High; and the time came that the Saints possessed the kingdom . . . And the kingdom and dominion, and the greatness of the kingdom under the whole heaven, shall be given to the people of the Saints of the Most High, Whose Kingdom is an Everlasting Kingdom, and all dominion shall serve and obey Him."** The Bible is clear that Jesus, along with his blood bought Saints will overcome this beast. Even better, it says in **Daniel 8:25** about Antichrist that, **". . . he shall also stand up against the Prince of princes** (Jesus); **but he shall be broken without hand."** The Saints will not even have to fight in the battle but will witness the destruction of Antichrist by the living Word of God, who is Jesus Christ!

In the next chapter, we will take a detailed look at Satan's secret army of men who have been used for nearly 500 years to bring about the New World Order and religion which he so desires in order to set himself up as the supreme god of this world. The Book of Daniel is so critical in identifying the Antichrist system and throughout history we have been able to see Satan's handiwork in the destruction of true Christianity and the formation of a world of people who ignore the commandments of God and worship the things of the world. These people believe *the lie of the serpent* in the Garden of Eden, **"You shall not surely die . . . (Genesis 3:4)."**

Chapter Five

SATAN'S SECRET MILITIA

The men of the Jesuit Order are most certainly *Satan's secret weapon* fighting against the truth found in God's Word. They are a *military religious order* of the Roman Catholic Church and are led by the Black Pope who is also called the "Jesuit General," a military name. They have become so powerful over the years that the Black Pope is now even more powerful than the White Pope of Rome. In 2013, a most interesting event occurred: the first ever Jesuit pope, Jorge Bergoglio, was elected into the Vatican and assumed the name of Pope Francis I. This historic appointment caused Bible prophecy scholars, who see the imminent threat of Rome, really perk up! We are now literally watching the fulfillment of the prophecies of the Book of Daniel and the Book of Revelation happen. The hour is short before the return of Jesus Christ!

I think it would be valuable to lay the foundation and the purpose of this Order. The Jesuit Order or the "Society of Jesus," began in 1540 by Ignatius Loyola as a counter-reformation for the Protestants who were leaving the Roman Catholic Church by the millions after Martin Luther sparked the Reformation of 1517. Up until this point in history, the Roman Catholic Church had kept its weary faithful in bondage claiming there was no salvation outside of their Church system and also forbidding the people to read the Word of God. It was Martin Luther, a Roman Catholic monk, who realized that "Mother Church" was not conformed to the Word of God, but to their own man made agenda. Many followed Martin Luther out of the Church of Rome and this infuriated Paul III, the reigning pope! Ignatius Loyola approached Pope Paul III and presented his idea to regain control of the Protestants and bring them back into the fold of Rome by using whatever means he would have to use to get them to comply. The Jesuit oath, written in the next paragraph, reveals some of these "means." Pope Paul III confirmed the Jesuit Order through the papal bull *Regimini militantis ecclesiae* meaning, "To the Government of the Church Militant", on September 27, 1540. The Jesuits were completely dedicated to the restoration of the pope's Universal Temporal and Spiritual Power. The Jesuit General's sole purpose is for the revival of the Roman Empire which is prophesied in Scripture to be the last Kingdom to gain control before the second coming of Jesus Christ. The headquarters of the society, its General Curia, is in Rome where Vatican City is located.[26]

The Jesuit oath reveals the sinister plotting and planning of the Jesuits to rid the world of "heretics" or "Protestants" by *any means necessary.* They are known for using mind control and hypnosis, as well as murder to subordinate their victims and to destroy the spread of "Protestantism." Please let me clarify that most people who would be considered to be "Protestants" by the pope of Rome would be true Bible believing Christians. Christians and Catholics are two very separate groups! True Christians believe that *Jesus saves* by His finished work on the Cross and true faithful Catholics believe that *the Church saves* by participating in their sacramental system.

A portion of the Jesuit oath reads: *"My son, heretofore you have been taught to act the dissembler: among Roman Catholics to be a Roman Catholic and to be a spy even among your own brethren; to believe no man, to trust no man. Among the Reformers, to be a reformer; among the Huguenots, to be a Huguenot; among the Calvinists, to be a Calvinist; among other Protestants, generally to be a Protestant, and obtaining their confidence, to seek even to preach from their pulpits, and to denounce with all the vehemence in your nature our Holy Religion and the pope; and even to descend so low as to become a Jew among Jews, that you might be enabled to gather together all*

---

[26] http://en.wikipedia.org/wiki/Society_of_Jesus

information for the benefit of your Order as a faithful soldier of the pope. You have been taught to insidiously plant the seeds of jealousy and hatred between communities, provinces, states that were at peace, and incite them to deeds of blood, involving them in war with each other, and to create revolutions and civil wars in countries that were independent and prosperous . . . To take sides with the combatants and to act secretly with your brother Jesuit, who might be engaged on the other side, but openly opposed to that with which you might be connected, only that the Church might be the gainer in the end, in the conditions fixed in the treaties for peace and that the end justifies the means. You have been taught your duty as a spy, to gather all statistics, facts and information in your power from every source; to ingratiate yourself into the confidence of the family circle of Protestants and heretics of every class and character, as well as that of the merchant, the banker, the lawyer, among the schools and universities, in parliaments and legislatures, and the judiciaries and councils of state, and to be all things to all men, for the pope's sake, whose servants we are unto death. I furthermore promise and declare that I will, when opportunity present, make and wage relentless war, secretly or openly, against all heretics, Protestants and Liberals, as I am directed to do, to extirpate and exterminate them from the face of the whole earth; and that I will spare neither age, sex or condition; and that I will hang, waste, boil, flay, strangle and bury alive these infamous heretics, rip up the stomachs and wombs of their women and crush their infants' heads against the walls, in order to annihilate forever their execrable race. That when the same cannot be done openly, I will secretly use the poisoned cup, the strangulating cord, the steel of the poniard or the leaden bullet, regardless of the honor, rank, dignity, or authority of the person or persons, whatever may be their condition in life, either public or private, as I at any time may be directed so to do by any agent of the pope or Superior of the Brotherhood of the Holy Faith, of the Society of Jesus."[27] Horrendous, right?

Another part of the Jesuit oath states, *"You must serve . . . as the instrument and executioner as directed by your superiors; for none can command here who has not consecrated his labors with the BLOOD of the heretic; for 'without the shedding of blood no man can be saved.'"* This is frighteningly similar to the Scripture in **Hebrews 9:22** which states, **". . . without shedding of blood, there is no remission (of sin)."** This is speaking of the precious blood of Jesus which took away the sin of the world, not the blood of murdered "heretics!"

The oath ends with the superior instructing the candidate to: *"Go ye, then, into all the world and take possession of all lands in the name of the pope. He who will not accept him as the Vicar of Jesus and his Vice-regent on earth, let him be accursed and exterminated."* Quite different than the Great Commission given by Jesus to His Disciples where it says, **"Go ye into all the world, and preach the Gospel to every creature (Luke 16:15)!"** The word "Gospel" simply means "The good news," which was that Jesus had defeated Satan, sin and death on the Cross.

Each individual Jesuit must first have trained as a priest, but is not required to remain in active clerical duties. After training, many are sent out on missions requiring them to be lawyers, doctors, teachers, journalist, bankers, and any vocation which will put them in position to further the aims of the Order. They are essentially "undercover agents" of the Jesuit General. Some will keep their title as a priest and they are usually the visible ones which put the initials "S.J." after their name signifying that they are a member of the "Society of Jesus."

Through Ignatius Loyola's *Spiritual Exercises*, the Jesuits strongly incorporate *hypnosis* into their practices. We have now read the bloody and binding Jesuit oath and it is hard to imagine how a person could carry out some of the devilish schemes required by the Superiors under the Jesuit General. In this next quote, we see precisely how it is done; *through using hypnosis*! H. Beohmer says in his book *Les Jesuits*, "We imbue unto him [a Jesuit initiate] spiritual forces, which he would find very difficult to eliminate later . . . These forces can come up again to the surface, sometime after years of not even mentioning them and become so imperative that the will [of the Jesuit] finds itself unable to oppose any obstacle and has to follow their irresistible impulse."[28] This shows that when a Jesuit is inducted into the Order, he is placed under hypnotic processes and occult spiritual forces which can be invoked at any time in the future to compel him to do the bidding of his Superiors.

---

[28] *Les Jesuits*, H. Beohmer, 1928, page 34-35

James White, a noted hypnotist, explains the power of the hypnotic induction, "The hypnotized may fall hopeless victims to the most criminal and harmful actions, not only while they sleep, but after they have been awakened. There lies such infernal power in the hands of the hypnotizer that everyone ought to be strictly forbidden to meddle with hypnotism, except those who are honorable and trustworthy. The hypnotized can by all kinds of suggestions be made not only to harm themselves, but also others, and they may even be irresistibly driven to any crime."[29]

A Jesuit must undertake the *Spiritual Exercises* created by Loyola. During the 30-day initiation rite of passage, the novice is told "what to think, how to feel, when to groan, how to sigh and what to imagine."[30] Loyola's meditation encourages visualization or imaging with the intended effect being *a mental transformation or a subtle reprogramming of the mind.* The *Spiritual Exercises* include frequent repetition of "Anima Christi," which was Loyola's own habitual prayer or mantra for *sensory deprivation.* The aim of the altered consciousness or sensory deprivation is for the total domination of the individual's mind by spiritual forces. By the means of this most subtle form of hypnosis, the mind of the Jesuit is reoriented, reprogrammed and altered. What you have left is essentially a walking, talking human robot programmed to do whatever his Superior requires!

During the time in history when the Jesuit Order was being conceived and groomed, there were also two other weapons used by Rome in their counter-reformation. One such weapon was the Council of Trent where the Roman Catholic Church pronounced hundreds of "anathemas" against the "heretics," which excommunicated them from the Church of Rome and condemned them to Hell for all of eternity. Some of these "anathemas" were for not believing in the "real presence" of Jesus in the Roman Catholic Eucharist, but only believing communion to be symbolic of the death of Christ. Others were for believing that one can be saved by faith in Jesus alone and not through the sacraments of the Roman Catholic Church. The Jesuits and the popes also used the many inquisitions to intimidate and kill "heretics" and "Protestants." They

---

[29] *Past, Present and Future*, James E. White, 1909, page 338-341
[30] *Codeword Barbelon*, P.D. Stuart, Lux-Verbi Books, 2009, page 118

burned men and woman at the stake, even using them as human burning lanterns on the street posts. The heinous ways that the non-Catholics were killed were gruesome and cruel to say the least. *Foxes Book of Martyrs* bears out some of the most sadistic ways that these ungodly men took the precious lives of those who would not bow to Rome. The inquisitions were sometimes carried out below ground in Vatican City. Charles Spurgeon wrote in his 1873 novel, *The Sword and the Trowel*. "They invented ovens, or furnaces, which being made red-hot, they lowered the condemned into them, bound hand and foot and immediately closed over them the mouth of the furnace." He goes on to write, "and in 1849, these furnaces at Rome were laid open to the public view in the dungeons of the holy Roman Inquisition near the great church of the Vatican, still containing the calcined bones." In a sermon, Charles Spurgeon said, "popery is abhorred of the Lord, and they who help it wear the Mark of the Beast . . ."[31]

The reality that the Jesuits, along with the pope, were on killing spree during this time caused many true Christians to flee to a new country to avoid the same fate. This is how America was founded; by people who were seeking to create a place where they could freely worship Jesus Christ without the fear of being killed. In 1620, the pilgrims landed at Plymouth Rock and the Jesuits, in disguise as Protestants, followed. Some were in the second ships to arrive on the shores of the United States and began a plan to destroy the new country from the inside out.[32] Their plan is very close to fulfillment right now. No one can deny that our beautiful country is being destroyed right before our very eyes.

Here is a quote by former Jesuit, Alberto Rivera, written before his death in the introduction to Edmond Paris' book, *The Secret History of the Jesuits*: "By the time Ignatius de Loyola arrived on the scene, the Protestant Reformation had seriously damaged the Roman Catholic system. Ignatius de Loyola came to the conclusion that the only way his 'Church' could survive was by enforcing the canons and doctrines on the temporal power of the pope and the Roman Catholic institution; not by just destroying the physical life of the people alone as the Dominican priests were doing through the Inquisition, *but by*

---

31 *The Metropolitan Tabernacle Pulpit Sermons*, parts 261-272, page 574
32 *Smokescreens*, Jack Chick, Chick Publications, 1983

infiltration and penetration into every sector of life. Protestantism must be conquered and used for the benefit of the popes. That was Ignatius de Loyola's personal proposal, among others, to Pope Paul III. Jesuits immediately went to work secretly infiltrating ALL Protestant groups including families, places of work, hospitals, schools, colleges, etc. Today, the Jesuits have almost completed that mission. The Bible puts the power of the local Church into the hands of a Godly pastor. But the cunning Jesuits successfully managed over the years to remove that power into the hands of denomination headquarters, and have now pushed almost all of the Protestant denominations into the arms of the Vatican. This is exactly what Ignatius de Loyola set out to accomplish: a universal Church and the end of Protestantism (my italics)."[33] Rivera goes onto write, "As you read *The Secret History of the Jesuits*, you will see there is a parallel between the religious and political sectors. The author, Mr. Paris, reveals the penetration and infiltration of the Jesuits into the governments and nations of the world to manipulate the course of history by setting up dictatorships, and weakening democracies such as the United States of America, by paving the way for social, political, moral, military, educational and religious anarchy."[34] Let us look at the power and influence the Jesuits have worldwide and in the United States of America, specifically. The phrase, "All roads lead to Rome" will make a whole lot more sense when you see that no matter where you look, they have planted themselves there and managed to move their way to the top.

The Jesuit symbol is "IHS" in the shape of a sunburst and represents the Egyptian pagan trinity; Isis, Horus and Seb. This is none other than sun worship which is also known as Baal worship! Please remember that this all began at the Tower of Babel and has never disappeared. It is Satan worship!

---

[33] *The Secret History of the Jesuits*, Introduction by Alberto Rivera, Chick Publications, translated from French 1975

[34] *The Secret History of the Jesuits*, Introduction by Alberto Rivera, Chick Publications, translated from French 1975

The Roman Catholic monstrance, an ornate vessel to house the consecrated Eucharist, which faithful Roman Catholics believe to literally be the body of Jesus Christ, is always in the shape of a sunburst.

Here are just *some* of the Papal Maxims of the Jesuits:[35]

#8. If Christ commands one thing, and the Pope another thing, *the Pope is rather to be obeyed than Jesus Christ.*

#9. The Pope's decretory letters are to be received and esteemed as authentic as the Word of God or the Holy Scriptures.

#11. If the Pope affirm that to be black, which our eyes judge to be white, we ought also to declare, that it's black, upon the pain of our souls.

#12. The Pope has the sole rule and power over the whole world in Temporals as well as in Spirituals, and therefore can depose (kill) Emperors and Kings . . .

#19. All Protestants are heretics, and therefore they ought to be killed.

Karl Marx, the father of modern Communism, was trained by the Jesuits inside the British Museum in 1848.[36] His goal was to bring about atheistic beliefs and to abolish the Bible in order to redefine the thinking of the people. In his 10th plank of *The Communist Manifesto* he stated about public schools, ". . . this is no mistake; if you control the education,

35 *Vatican Assassins,* Eric Phelps, page 10
36 *Codeword Barbelon,* P. D. Stuart, Lux-Verbi Books, 2009, page 196

you control the people."[37] The Jesuits are known for their obsession with education which may sound progressive to most people. However, the Jesuits can now freely brainwash children in the educational systems, and rewrite history as they have been doing for centuries.

Joseph Stalin, leader of the Soviet Union and founder of the Communist Party, was a Jesuit-trained Roman Catholic. He studied at the Jesuit seminary in Tiflis (Tblisis), Soviet Georgia, to be educated for the priesthood.[38] The Communist Party was created by the Vatican to destroy one of its greatest enemies, the Russian Orthodox Church, whose members were called Serbians. However, the Communists betrayed the pope and refused to destroy the Orthodox Church. So under Pope Pius XII in the 1940's, the Roman Catholic priests changed out of their clerical robes and put on the uniform of the Ustashi where they went out and tortured, maimed and killed Serbian men, woman, and children.[39] One gruesome story is a story of a family who was taken by the priests of the Ustashi, and the father was separated from the mother and their four children. For seven days the mother and children were tortured with starvation and thirst. Finally, they brought the mother and children water and a nice sized roast which the family devoured. Not long after, the Ustashi told them that they had eaten the flesh of their father![40] This "forced conversion" program took the lives of over 840,000 souls.[41]

Speaking of the Ustashi, it was Adolf Hitler who put them into power in compliance with the Vatican's Third Reich Concordant of July 20, 1933.[42] Hitler, the Roman Catholic leader of the Nazi Party, once said about the Jesuit Order, "I learned much from the Order of the Jesuits. Until now, there has never been anything more grandiose, on the earth, than the hierarchal organization of the Catholic Church. I transferred much of this organization into my own party (the Nazi Party)."[43] Otto Strasser, one of the founders of the Nazi Party, and author of the

[37] http://christkeep.com/articles/jesuits_evolution.html
[38] *Codeword Barbelon,* P. D. Stuart, Lux-Verbi Books, 2009, page 196
[39] *Smokescreens,* Jack Chick, Chick Publications, 1983, page 25
[40] *Smokescreens,* Jack Chick, Chick Publications, 1983, page 32
[41] *Codeword Barbelon,* P. D. Stuart, Lux-Verbi Books, 2009, page 197
[42] *Codeword Barbelon,* P. D. Stuart, Lux-Verbi Books, 2009, page 197
[43] *Smokescreens,* Jack Chick, Chick Publications, 1983, page 20

book, *Hitler and I*, tells us that Hitler's famous book, *Mein Kampf* was ghostwritten by a Jesuit priest named Bernhardt Staempfle.[44] Even his speeches were scripted by the Jesuits!

Hitler appointed the notorious, Heinrich Himmler, a Jesuit priest, as the commander of the special elite corps known as the S.S.[45] Hitler said of Himmler, "I can see Himmler as our Ignatius Loyola."[46] Himmler not only ordered the killings of multiple millions, but also demanded to see pictures of the tortured and dead; a kind of "keep sake" for him. Walter Schellenberg, a former chief of the German counter-espionage under Hitler admitted after the war, "The S.S. organization had been constituted by Himmler, according to the principles of the Jesuit Order. Their regulations and the *Spiritual Exercises* prescribed by Ignatius Loyola were the model Himmler tried to copy exactly."[47]

Hitler was a faithful Roman Catholic until his death. On the day of his supposed suicide, May 3, 1945, the following eulogy was published in honor of him: "Adolf Hitler, son of the Catholic Church, died while defending Christianity [Catholicism] . . . words cannot be found to lament over his death . . . Over his mortal remains stands his victorious moral figure. With the palm of the martyr God gives Hitler the laurels of Victory."[48]

Many have wondered how Hitler, a German corporal without a prestigious title or position managed to get himself appointed as head of the powerful nation of Germany. The answer is well given by British Historian, Alan Bullock, where he says, "Hitler came into office in 1933 as the result, not of any irresistible revolutionary or national movement sweeping him into power, nor even of a popular victory at the polls, but as a part of a shoddy political deal with the 'Old Gang' . . . Hitler did not seize power; he was jobbed into office by a backstairs intrigue."[49] I take

---

[44] *Hitler and I,* Otto Strasser, Houghton Miflin, 1940, page 57
[45] *Codeword Barbelon,* P. D. Stuart, Lux-Verbi Books, 2009, page 206
[46] *Libres Propos,* Adolf Hitler, Flammarion, 1952, page 164
[47] *Le Chef de Contre-Espionage Nazi Vous Parie,* Walter Schellenberg, Julliard, 1957, page 23-24
[48] *Secret History of the Jesuits, page 162*
[49] *Hitler, A Study in Tyranny,* Alan Bullock, Viking Press, 1952, page 213

the time to ask this question and reveal this response as a comparison of how the President of the United States, Barack Obama, was swiftly put into power out of nowhere. Before the election, he was not at all well known to the public and only spent a little over a hundred days as a United States Senator before he rose to be the top Democratic candidate for President of the United States of America. The question is: Was he too part of a "shoddy political deal" and "jobbed into office by a backstage intrigue"?

Does Barack Obama have any Jesuit connections? It is no secret that Obama worked extensively in community organizing in the 1980's. But what is not so well known is that Obama was hired by a Catholic lay minister, Jerry Kellman, as lead organizer for a Chicago organization called the "Developing Communities Project," funded by Chicago's south-side Catholic Churches. Surprised? Here is a little more information linking Obama to the Roman Catholic Church and the Jesuits: Obama's Chicago mentor was Gregory Galluzzo, a Jesuit priest! His chief speechwriter is Jon Favreau, a Jesuit-trained "ethics" professor; Obama's Senior Military and Foreign Policy Advisor is Jesuit-trained Major General J. Scott Gration; His Deputy Communications Director, Dan Pfeiffer, is Jesuit-trained; and I must mention the fact that Barack Obama chose Jesuit controlled Joe Biden as his vice president.[50] Father Charles L. Currie, president of the Association of Jesuit Colleges and Universities (AJCU), is a speaker for the "Catholics in Alliance for the Common Good (CACG)." The association discloses that: Eight alumni of the 28 Jesuit colleges and universities currently serve in appointed positions to U.S. President Barack Obama's administration and fifty two alumni are current members of the 111th U.S. Congress. Members of the Obama administration from AJCU institutions include Central Intelligence Agency Director Leon E. Panetta (Santa Clara University, 1960, BA) and Department of Defense Secretary Robert M. Gates (Georgetown University, 1974, PhD). [51]

Fidel Castro of communist Cuba was trained by the Jesuits for 7 years and he is a Roman Catholic Jesuit "lay brother."[52] He was educated

---

[50] *Codeword Barbelon*, P. D. Stuart, Lux-Verbi Books, 2009, page 183

[51] http://www.usasurvival.org/docs/Global_Religion.pdf

[52] *Vatican Assassins*, Eric Jon Phelps, page 253

at various Jesuit schools, one being El Colegio de Belen, a Jesuit boarding school in Havana. Cuba is his Jesuit kindergarten, where he teaches Cuban citizens the Jesuit principles. Yasser Arafat, the creator of the Palestinian Liberation Organization, also known as the PLO, was also trained by the Jesuits. The supposed Jewish Zionist movement is under the Jesuit General as well, making people believe that the Jews of the world are plotting a takeover! The Zionist movement is a smokescreen like so many other Jesuit created distractions.

The Jesuits also founded and control the Council on Foreign Relations.[53] Almost all directors and seats on the CFR are Roman Catholic Jesuit-trained individuals and anyone who aligns themselves with this organization is most likely "one of them" as well.

The Jesuits are directly linked to the European Union through a group known as OCIPE. This is a group of Jesuits "who share their intelligence with the European Union."[54] Both headquarters are located in Brussels, Belgium. The EU motto is "Unity in Diversity." They make no apologies about their goal to reverse what God did at the Tower of Babel. God scattered the people which ultimately formed different nations, but the EU is attempting to bring the nations together again. In front of the European Union Parliament building is Strasburg, France, there is a stature of a woman riding on the back of a beast just like the prophecy in **Revelation 17:3** which describes the false religious system and the Antichrist! The EU elected Jesuit-educated Herman van Rompuy as its first full-time president. The artist, Pieter Breugel the Elder in 1563, created a depiction of the Tower of Babel and it is a very close match to the intentional unfinished architecture of the EU office in Brussels, Belgium.

---

[53]   http://www.vaticanassassins.org/?p=272
[54]   http://www.jesuit.org.uk/faithandjustice/frankturner1.htm

| Artist depiction of the Tower of Babel | European Union office in Brussels, Belgium |

The Jesuits are known to control the infamous Bilderberg Group which held its first highly secretive meeting in the Bilderberg Hotel of the Netherlands in 1954. The group was founded by Jesuit Joseph Rettinger, who also founded the EU.[55] The Bilderberg Group is a collection of approximately 130 influential businessmen, financiers and politicians who meet once a year at an invitation-only conference.[56]

Now, let us take a look at the influence of the Jesuit Order in the United States of America. There is a Jesuit quotation which states, *"We are also determined to take possession of the United States; but we must proceed with the utmost secrecy."*[57]

We have already exposed that the Jesuits are a power force beyond description and that they despise "Protestants" with every fiber of their being. We know these facts because of the Jesuit oath and because they have continually tried to destroy the "heretics" of the Roman Catholic Church and any form of freedom that these people may have. The Jesuits also despise the United States of America and what it stands for, namely "freedom of liberty." They desire the opposite of freedom which is fascism and they want the entire population of the world to be under subjection to their system. What kind of power and authority do the Jesuits and the Roman Catholic Church have on our United States government?

---

[55] http://en.wikipedia.org/wiki/Joseph_Retinger

[56] http://www.rinf.com/columnists/news/10-secret-societies-you-need-to-know-about

[57] http://www.pacinst.com/terrorists/chapter3/htb.html

Would you believe that Washington D.C. was once a city called *Rome, Mary*land? A Jesuit-trained Roman Catholic named Daniel Carroll, brother of Jesuit John Carroll, was put in charge of finding a place for the nation's capital, and in 1790 he found Rome, Maryland to be the perfect spot![58] Of course, Vatican City is located in Rome, Italy. Is that a mere coincidence? Notice the similar architecture on the picture of the Vatican compared to a picture of Capitol Hill located in Washington, D.C.

Also, see the bronze statue of Persephone on top of the Capitol Dome. She is the Greek Goddess of the Immaculate Conception, or the "Virgin Mary" of the Roman Catholic Church. This was designed by a Roman Catholic named Thomas Crawford in Rome.

The Egyptian obelisk is also a pagan phallic symbol which was sometimes called the "Baal Shaft." This derives from the fertility cults

---

58 http://en.ikipedia.org/wiki/Rome,_Maryland

which worshipped the male reproductive organ because it creates life. An obelisk is found prominently displayed in St. Peter's Square in Vatican City, Rome. The Washington Monument in Washington, D.C. is also shaped like an Egyptian obelisk.

The *Roman* fasces are a symbol of authority, where the word "fascism" is derived. It is displayed openly in our U. S. House of Representatives where any and all decisions are made which affect our nation and its citizens. In his book, *The Rulers of Evil,* Tupper Saussy says, ". . . the House Fasces represent the Black Pope (the Jesuit General) who indeed rules the world."

This symbol is that of the Knights of Columbus fraternity with the Roman fasces in the middle. The Knights of Columbus was formed in 1882 as an American Roman Catholic fraternity.[59] It was founded by a Jesuit priest named Michael J. McGivney.[60] At the fourth degree the Knights of Columbus member takes the same oath that the Jesuits do. There are more than 1.7 million members in 14,000 councils, with nearly 200 councils on college campuses.[61] These men were affectionately called by Pope John Paul II, "The right lay arm of the Catholic Church in America" and they are committed to bringing back the Universal Temporal Power to the pope of Rome and even pledge their allegiance to him *over* the United States Constitution.[62] Their catch phrase is "MAC," which means "Make America Catholic." In their oath, they commit themselves to be killed or destroyed if they fail to comply.[63]

This is a quotation found in *The Suppressed Truth About the Assassination of Abraham Lincoln*, where it says, "During the Wilson administrations the Army, the Navy, the Treasury, the Secret Service, the Post Office, the Emergency Fleet, Transports, Printing, Aircraft and dozens of others were presided over by Fourth Degree Knights of Columbus [who take the same deadly oath as the Jesuits]!"[64] As anyone can see, the Knights of Columbus play a very critical role in the takeover of America, with very few people understanding their power and motives!

Former priest, Jeremiah Crowley, explains the true purpose of the Knights of Columbus when he writes, "The Knights themselves . . . are heart and soul in politics. This fact is well known to political machines

[59]   http://en.wikipedia.org/wiki/Knights_of_Columbus
[60]   http://catholic-saints.suite101.com/article.cfm/fr_michael_j_mcgivney
[61]   http://en.wikipedia.org/wiki/Knights_of_Columbus
[62]   *Smokescreens,* Jack Chick, Chick Publications, 1983, page 85
[63]   *Smokescreens,* Jack Chick, Chick Publications,1983, page 83
[64]   *The Suppressed Truth About the Assassination of Abraham Lincoln*, Burke McCarty, Arya Varta Publishing Co., 1973;(first published in 1924) pages 23, 239

and non-Catholic politicians, whose candidates must receive the approval of Rome and the Knights before they dare nominate them for either dog pound or presidency. Knights of Columbus have assured me that their organization, with the Church of Rome, controls the Municipal, State and Federal Government, and also influences the business interests throughout the country. They have also assured me within the past few years (1900-12) that it is almost impossible for a man to secure a position or promotion in any business house or corporation, if a Knight of Columbus be a competitor. Notwithstanding these facts, the innocent Knights, like their Jesuitical advisors, publicly declare that they are not in politics, as the rules of their organization forbid their being in such an unholy environment . . . [*Their*] principal business is politics, aye, Jesuitical politics, which has been the curse of Catholic countries, and is today a menace to non-Catholic countries . . . Rome's Jesuitical emissaries, agents and missionaries are everywhere. They have no conscience but the Pope's dictation . . . Their object is to engender strife, to influence party spirit, to produce faction, to counsel rebellion, to plot and plan assassinations."[65] The Knights of Columbus have certainly been underestimated by the average person here in America!

The Jesuits set up the Federal Reserve Bank in 1913 as a means to control the economy here in the United States and also to create more money for their Order. The Federal Reserve is not a "federal" agency as its name suggests, but is a privately owned corporation run by very powerful individuals. Under President Richard Nixon in 1971, the United States was taken off of the gold standard which kept checks and balances on our nation's debt. Now, our privately owned Federal Reserve can print billions of dollars out of thin air! As a result, the value of the American dollar has declined greatly and we are now in the worst debt we have ever faced as a nation.

These three famous financial families: the Rothschilds, the Morgans, and the Rockefellers all do the bidding of the Jesuit Order because of Jesuit infiltration in their organizations, even to this very day. They do whatever is necessary to destroy constitutional liberty in America. Many times, there were attempts to create a *central bank* in the United States

---

[65] Romanism: A Menace to the Nation, Jeremiah J. Crowley, The Menace Publishing Co., 1912, pages 157, 158, 136

but each time it failed because of fraudulent activities on the part of the bankers, but also because of the careful attention of some influential and honest Americans, such as millionaire, John Jacob Astor, and others who would not succumb to the bullies of the Vatican.

There was a third attempt to create a central banking system pushed by the Rothschild banking dynasty. One of the founders of the Masters of the Illuminati was Mayer Amschel Bauer, who later changed his last name to Rothschild. He was the money man behind the public founder, Jesuit Adam Weishaupt![66] Also, the Rothschild family bears the name of "Guardian of the Vatican Treasury."[67] It was the Rothschilds and Jacob Schiff, a Jesuit, who sought to gain control of the banking system of the United States. The Jesuits and the Rothschilds believe that "he who has the gold, makes the rules." [68] This is their *golden rule*! This attempt at a central bank eventually failed too under Andrew Jackson, but in 1913, they were finally able to create a central bank in the United States of America. They named their magic money machine "The Federal Reserve Bank."

The Federal Reserve has the power to print money with nothing as collateral, lend it to the banks and then charge interest to the banks for money which never did even exist! Not only does the interest earned go into the pockets of the already filthy rich, but this causes *inflation* for the American people, *enormous debt* for our nation and the *decline of the value of the American dollar*, which is exactly what would cause the economic collapse of a world super-power such as the United States of America; a goal of the Jesuits and the pope of the Roman Catholic Church ever since the inception of this great country!

The *Constitution of the United States* gave Congress the power to coin money. If Congress coined its own money, as the *Constitution* directs, it would not have to pay the hundreds of billions of dollars of interest that it now pays each year to the bankers for the national debt. Andrew Jackson, who greatly opposed a central bank said, "If Congress has the right under the Constitution to issue paper money, it was given to be used by

---

[66]   http://www.cuttingedge.org/News/n2020.cfm
[67]   *Rulers of Evil,* F. Tupper Saussy, Harper Collins, page 160, 161
[68]   http://www.pacinst.com/terrorists/chapter2/jackson.html

themselves, not to be delegated to individuals or corporations."[69] Thomas Jefferson said, "The central bank is an institution of the most deadly hostility existing against the principles and form of our Constitution . . . If the American people allow private banks to control the issuance of their currency, first by inflation and then by deflation, the banks and corporations that will grow up around them will deprive the people of all their property until their children will wake up homeless on the continent their fathers conquered."[70]

Let us dig a little deeper into the formation of the Federal Reserve Bank. As I already stated, there were many who opposed the forming of a central bank and that is why it took four attempts to finally get the votes needed to implement it. What finally changed the minds of the ones opposing the Federal Reserve Bank? Well, to put it plainly, *a dead man* has no opinion or no vote for that matter. How in the world would the Jesuits pull this off without anyone suspecting them? What you will read here shows the absolute mastermind of these individuals. They have the intellect, the boldness and the money to do whatever necessary to put their plan of world domination into effect.

In April of 1912, the "unsinkable" *Titanic* would serve as a death ship for those who opposed the Jesuits' plan for a central bank. This floating palace was created to be the tomb for the wealthy who stood in the way of the Jesuit General. Ironically, after *the Titanic* sank in 1912, *all opposition to the Federal Reserve was eliminated* and by December of 1913, the Jesuits finally had there long sought after central bank!

Sinking a multi-million dollar ship and the loss of thousands of innocent and unsuspecting lives were worth it all because their plan worked perfectly. If you fast forward almost 100 years, the Federal Reserve Bank is running like the corrupt machine it was made to be. We are in *dire straits* financially as a nation, and it is *not by accident*! For the Jesuits, it is all about *money, power and **control**.*

I am sure some may doubt this "conspiracy theory," so let me expound with a little more proof. Remember, there were a number of very

69   http://quotes.liberty-tree.ca/quotes_by/andrew+jackson
70   http://www.phnet.fi/public/mamaa1/jefferson.htm

wealthy and powerful men who made it abundantly clear that they were not in favor of the Federal Reserve Bank. These men would have been able to block the establishment of the Federal Reserve so they had to be destroyed by a means so preposterous that no one would suspect that they were actually *murdered* in a cold and calculated way; and certainly no one would suspect the Jesuits.

J.P. Morgan, which is controlled by the Jesuits, owned the international shipping trust, *White Star Line*, which built *the Titanic*. The Jesuits had ordered J. P. Morgan to build this luxury passenger-liner steamship. In order to further shield the papacy and the Jesuits from suspicion, many Irish, French, and Italian Roman Catholics immigrating to the New World were aboard. In the eyes of the Jesuits, these people were expendable because "the end justifies the means." Protestants from Belfast who wanted to immigrate to the United States were also invited on board.

All of the wealthy and powerful men whom the Jesuits wanted to dispose of were invited on this famous voyage. Three of the richest and most important of these men were: Benjamin Guggenheim; Isador Strauss, the head of Macy's Department Stores; and John Jacob Astor who was probably the wealthiest man in the world at that time. Their total wealth, at that time, using dollar values of their day was more than 500 million dollars. Today that amount of money would be worth nearly eleven billion dollars. These three men were coaxed and encouraged to board the floating palace. They had to be destroyed because the Jesuits knew that they would use their wealth and influence to oppose a Federal Reserve Bank, as well as, the various wars which were being planned.

Edward Smith was the captain of *the Titanic*. He had been traveling the North Atlantic waters for twenty-six years and was the world's most experienced master of the North Atlantic routes. He had also worked for J.P. Morgan for many years. Edward Smith was a Jesuit Temporal Coadjutor and served the Jesuit Order as a sea captain.[71] It was not "by accident" that *the Titanic* ran head on and full speed into an iceberg!

---

[71] *The Secret Terrorist*, Bill Hughes

It is a well-known fact that there were not enough life boats on the ship. It is difficult to believe that this ship had every luxury you could dream of in the early 1900's; including a gymnasium, swimming pools, a squash court, Turkish baths, a library, barber shops, but they could not afford enough life boats?[72] That seems like a very unlikely scenario! Those behind the creation of *the Titanic* knew of the rule of protocol, "woman and children first" in a crisis and they knew that most of the heroic men would adhere to that rule. Also, to prevent nearby freighters from responding for help, white flares were sent up instead of red flares. White flares to a passing freightliner just meant that everyone was having a party![73]

Many interesting and revealing points about *the Titanic* were discussed in a video created by National Geographic in 1986. This video was entitled, "The Secrets of the Titanic." When *the Titanic* departed from Southern England on April 10, 1912, Jesuit Provincial Francis Browne, the Superior of Captain Edward Smith, boarded *the Titanic*. This man was the most powerful Jesuit in all of Ireland and answered directly to the Jesuit General in Rome. The videotape declares, "A vacationing priest, Father Francis Browne, caught these poignant snapshots of his fellow passengers, most of them on a voyage to eternity. The next day *the Titanic* made her last stop off the coast of Queenstown, Ireland. Here tenders brought out the last passengers; mostly Irish immigrants headed for new homes in America. *And here, the lucky Father Browne disembarked . . . .* Father Browne caught Captain Smith peering down from Titanic's bridge, poised on the brink of destiny (my italics)."[74] "Here is Jesuit treachery at its finest. The Provincial [Father Francis Browne—a high ranking Jesuit] boards *the Titanic*, photographs the victims, most assuredly briefs the Captain concerning his oath as a Jesuit, and the following morning bids him farewell."[75] Edward Smith knew that he would be a victim, as well, but because he believed that the Jesuit General is the representative of God, he was willing to lose his life to win a great victory for his Order.

---

[72]   http://en.wikipedia.org/wiki/RMS_Titanic#Features

[73]   http://www.pacinst.com/terrorists/chapter5/titanic.html

[74]   *The Secrets of the Titanic*, National Geographic video, 1986.

[75]   *Vatican Assassins*, Eric J. Phelps, page 427

As a result of the sinking of *the Titanic* and the silence of the opposition who perished in the freezing waters of the North Atlantic; in December of 1913, the Federal Reserve Bank was finally approved in the United States. Eight short months later, the Jesuits had sufficient funding through the Federal Reserve Bank to begin World War I.[76]

Prior to this time, Jesuit Jacob Schiff had been assigned the task of taking over the American banking system and establishing the Federal Reserve in the late 1800's with orders from the Rothschild dynasty. By the turn of the twentieth century, Schiff had control of the entire banking fraternity on Wall Street.[77] This was monumental because having control over the financial aspect of America gave them incredible power to control the destiny of America's future.

According to former Jesuit, Alberto Rivera, the Jesuits actually desire *anarchy and rioting* to be able to implement their plan for martial law and for a final take over. Martial law is the system of rules which takes effect when the military takes control of the normal administration of justice.[78] Oliver North directly helped draft a plan in 1984 to impose martial law in the United States in the event of an emergency. This secret plan would suspend the U.S. Constitution and turn over control of the government to FEMA (Federal Emergency Management Agency). This plan would appoint *military commanders* to run state and local governments. Implementation of this plan would have been triggered by violent and wise spread internal dissent, disagreement with government policy or national opposition to any U.S. military invasion abroad. Essentially, it amounts to a complete and total suspension of the U.S. Constitution and Bill of Rights.[79]

What is the Federal Emergency Management Agency (FEMA)? *Simply put, it is the "secret government."* This agency has powers and authority that go well beyond any other agency in the nation. What can FEMA do? It can suspend laws; Move entire populations; Arrest and detain citizens without a warrant and can hold them without

[76] http://www.pacinst.com/terrorists/chapter5/titanic.html
[77] Lecture by Myron Fagan, *The Illuminati and the Council on Foreign Relations*
[78] http://en.wikipedia.org/wiki/Martial_law
[79] http://www.newswithviews.com/Devvy/kidd394.htm

a trial; Seize property, food supplies, and transportation systems; and even suspend the *Constitution of the United States*. The original public mission of FEMA was to assure the survivability of the United States government in the event of a nuclear attack. The secondary function was to be a federal coordinating body during times of domestic disasters, such as, earthquakes, floods, and hurricanes. A series of Executive Orders was used to create FEMA. Unfortunately, it does not matter whether an Executive Order is constitutional or not, it simply becomes law by being published in the Federal Registry!

Here is an explanation of some of the Executive Orders which give FEMA the power to carry out these plans:[80]

- *Executive Order Number 10990*: Allows the government to take control over all modes of transportation, highways and seaports.
- *Executive Order Number 10995*: Allows the government to seize and control the communications media.
- *Executive Order Number 10997*: Allows the government to take over all electrical power, gas, petroleum, fuels and minerals.
- *Executive Order Number 10998*: Allows the government to take over all food resources and farms.
- *Executive Order Number 11000*: Allows the government to mobilize civilians into work brigades under government supervision.
- *Executive Order Number 11001*: Allows the government to take over all health, education and welfare functions.
- *Executive Order Number 11002*: Designates the Postmaster General to operate national registration of all persons.
- *Executive Order Number 11003*: Allows the government to take over all airports and aircraft, including commercial aircraft.
- *Executive Order Number 11004*: Allows the Housing and Financing Authority to relocate communities, build new housing with public funds, designate areas to be abandoned, and establish new locations for populations.
- *Executive Order Number 11005*: Allows the government to take over all railroads, inland waterways and public storage facilities.

80   http://www.freedomfiles.org/war/fema.htm

- *Executive Order Number 11051*: Specifies the responsibility of the Office of Emergency Planning and gives authorization to put all Executive Orders into effect in times of increased international tensions and economic or financial crisis.
- *Executive Order Number 11310*: Grants authority to the Department of Justice to enforce the plans set out in Executive Orders, to institute industrial support, to establish judicial and legislative liaison, to control all aliens, to operate penal and correctional institutions, and to advise and assist the President.
- *Executive Order Number 11921*: Allows the Federal Emergency Preparedness Agency to develop plans to establish control over the mechanisms of production and distribution, of energy sources, wages, salaries, credit and flow of money in the U.S.A. financial institution in any undefined national emergency. It also provides that when a state of emergency is declared by the President, Congress cannot review the action for six months.

What is even more frightening is the massive number of FEMA camps which are located all across the U.S. The government has taken abandoned train stations, airport parking lots, former military bases and industrial complexes and they have installed layers of fencing, coded areas and the only way in and out of the facility is through the electronic turnstiles surrounded by prison bars. The barbed wire on the fences faces inward not outward, meaning that it is not put there to keep intruders from getting inside the facility but it put there to keep the inhabitants from getting out! There are also security cameras installed where there were not previously and helicopter wind socks.[81]

Why are these camps of such concern? Because President Obama signed the *National Defense Authorization Act (NDAA)* into law which in addition to allocating $662 billion to the Pentagon, also contains a measure which allows U.S. citizens to be taken into custody and held indefinitely without ever being charged with a crime. Not only can any citizen deemed a threat to "national security interests of the United States," be held forever without receiving a trial, but the military will be the ones arresting those citizens. NDAA Section 1022, subsection C

---

[81] http://tellmenow.com/secret-fema-death-camps-already-at-a-location-near-you/

allows "(1) Detention under the law of war without trial until the end of the hostilities authorized by the Authorization for Use of Military Force." This law basically repeals habeas corpus, by not requiring the government to give cause or evidence as to why the person is being detained; the 6th Amendment which ensures U.S. citizens the right to counsel, as well as, the Posse Comitatus Act of 1878 which prevents federal military forces from being deployed and used against U.S. citizens.[82] Please look in this index of this book to view the FEMA camps designated in each state.

There are also pictures floating around the internet of plastic type caskets by the hundreds of thousands which have been shipped into America and are being stored all over the country.

Here is the caption provided under the previous image: *Plastic coffins and concentration camps—Just outside Atlanta, Georgia, beside a major road are approximately 500,000 plastic coffins. Stacked neatly and in full view, the coffins are allegedly owned by the Federal Emergency Management Agency (FEMA). Conspiracy theorists believe that FEMA has also set up several concentration camps in the US in preparation for the imposition of a state of martial law and the killing of millions of Americans. They suggest that the financial crisis will be used to justify the imposition of a police state (martial law).[83]*

82   http://www.thedailysheeple.com/find-the-fema-camp-nearest-you_062013

83   http://www.telegraph.co.uk/news/picturegalleries/howaboutthat/3477148/The-greatest-conspiracy-theories-in-history.html?image=4

Remember the concentration camps set up during World War II? These FEMA camps are nothing different, they will just be presented as "shelters for those in need" in the event of natural disasters or some cataclysmic event which would displace people from their homes. But, if that was the case then why are these facilities structured more like a prison with razor barbed wire fencing facing inward and no way in and out of the facility except through electronic turnstiles. This does not appear to be a voluntary shelter! There have been many disasters which have been perpetrated, including major oil spills and oil rig explosions, bombings, school shootings, and even earthquakes and weather events. Yes, they have even figured a way to manipulate the weather using HAARP towers! Of course, I do believe that God is in control, but these wicked people often get their way because of the sad fact that America is so steeped in sin that judgment is inevitable. God loved His chosen people, the Israelites, but because of their continual idolatry and backsliding, they were allowed to be taken as captives by other nations.

Earlier this year, the military distributed 165 surplus MRAPs to law enforcement agencies across the country. We are talking about massive bullet proof military vehicles which have no place in local police departments![84] Here was another current headline which shows the collaboration of military with local police forces: *US Army Special Forces Now Training with Local Police in Secret Joint Effort.* The article accurately states that this partnership is blurring the lines between the U.S. military and local sheriff departments and sets a dangerous precedent which erodes freedom and civil liberties.[85] Additionally, a very troubling report came out in August 2007, when KSLA-12 in Shreveport, Louisiana, reported that members of the clergy have been enrolled in a federal program which teach them how to "quell dissent" amongst their Church congregations. So-called "Clergy Response Teams" are reportedly being trained by FEMA to convince people to follow government orders in the event of martial law.

As anyone can clearly see, the Jesuits have managed to control it all: from the education system to the mainstream media; from the armed

---

[84] http://theadvocate.com/home/7684773-125/brpd-state-police-get-armored
[85] http://freedomoutpost.com/2014/01/us-army-special-forces-now-training-local-police-secret-joint-effort/

forces to the secret service; from the powerful secret societies to the local city police forces and not to mention the Federal Reserve! The only thing they do not completely have under their control yet is the land that stretches "from sea to shining sea." We, in the United States of America, are *the immediate target*. Will the people of America wake up in time?

Chapter Six

EXTINGUISHING THE LIGHT

It is terribly disheartening to witness what men, inspired by Satan, are capable of; but God continually warned us through His prophets and apostles of the impending deception. The Apostle Paul warned that after his departure **"grievous wolves (Acts 20:29)"** would come and lead the sheep astray. In **Acts 20:31** he said, **"Therefore watch, and remember, that by the space of three years I ceased not to warn everyone night and day with tears."** And in **2 Corinthians 2:17,** he warned of the many who would corrupt the Word of God saying, **"For we are not as many, which corrupt the Word of God: but as of sincerity, but as of God, in the sight of God speak we in Christ."** And Peter warned **2 Peter 2:1-2** saying, **"But there were false Prophets also among the people, even as there shall be false teachers among you, who privily shall bring in damnable heresies, even denying the Lord Who bought them, and bring upon themselves swift destruction. And many shall follow their pernicious ways; by reason of whom the way of Truth shall be evil spoken of."**

It is so very important to read and know the true Word of God because Satan is extremely deceptive! He will form a counterfeit Christ and a counterfeit Gospel to take people away from the true way of salvation, which is only by the blood that Jesus shed on the Cross to pay our sin debt. Jesus promised that His followers would be persecuted and even killed for His namesake. In **Matthew 24:9** He said, **"Then shall they deliver you up to be afflicted, and shall kill you."** And in **2 Timothy 3:12-13,** it is written, **"Yes, and all who will live Godly in Christ Jesus shall suffer persecution. But evil men and seducers shall wax worse and worse, deceiving and being deceived."**

Down through the centuries, Christians were tortured and killed by a succession of Roman Emperors. By 313 A.D., Roman Emperor Constantine would decree the Edict of Milan, mentioned in an earlier chapter. Of course, this proclamation resulted in the Church and state becoming one under the leadership of one man, who eventually became the "pope" by name. Constantine set himself up as the leader of this new Church. As head of the Pagan priesthood, he was the Pontifex Maximus and needed a similar title as head of this new universal Church. The people honored him as "Bishop of Bishops," while Constantine called himself the "vicar of Christ,"[86] which is still the official title of the pope of the Roman Catholic Church to this very day. This new weave of Christianity and pagan Roman traditions combined to form a universal Church which was named the "Catholic Church," because the word "catholic" means "universal." In 331 A.D., Constantine issued another edict that those who had not come under the authority of Rome would be arrested, persecuted and their Churches and Church records were to be burned. Those who opposed the new universal faith would be persecuted and killed. All in all, with Constantine's new edict, it is said that more Christians were persecuted and killed after his alleged conversion than before! The "universal" Catholic Church began becoming the wealthiest institution on the face of the Earth.[87] In around 354 A.D., Augustine stated that anything decreed by Rome was a closed matter. That was the power and authority this empire possessed!

The pope at this time was called "the Bishop of Rome"[88] or the "vicar of Christ."[89] The title "pope" was adopted around 600 A.D.[90] Specifically

---

[86] *A Woman Rides the Beast*, Dave Hunt, Harvest House Publishers, Oregon, 1994, page 46

[87] *A Woman Rides the Beast*, Dave Hunt, Harvest House Publishers, Oregon, 1994, page 76-77

[88] http://www.newadvent.org/cathen/12260a.htm

[89] http://www.newadvent.org/cathen/15403b.htm

[90] *The Evangelist*, December 2006 edition, page 10

in 606 A.D.; Roman Emperor Phocus made Pope Boniface III the Universal Bishop over all the Churches. This was when the papal power was officially established. Thomas Hobbes published in 1691, ". . . the Papacy is no other than the ghost of the deceased Roman Empire, sitting crowned upon the grave thereof."[91]

As a result of the marriage of Church and state, Bible believers began to be persecuted in the early century. Many fled to Europe and Asia Minor into the mountains to flee from persecution. These people were the true Church instituted by Jesus Himself and they looked upon Rome as Antichrist! Some of these people were the Waldenses and Albigenses who were forerunners to the great Reformers who succeeded them. They were true Christians defending their faith even until death. Jesus said in **John 16:2-4, ". . . yea, the time comes that whosoever kills you will think he does God a service. And these things they will do unto you, because they have not known the Father, nor Me. But these things I have told you, that when the time shall come, you may remember that I told you of them."**

The Dark Ages were named so because the Bible was forbidden among the people. **Psalms 119:105** says, **"Thy Word is a lamp unto my feet and a light unto my path."** In the 13th century, Rome made an effort to extinguish that light and to keep men from the knowledge of the Scriptures. A Catholic priest named Dominic Guzman and Pope Innocent III began the awful inquisitions threatening death to anyone who possessed the Bible. This began with the Albigenses in France. Dominic would often debate with Albigenses and said himself of them, "It is not by the display of power and pomp, or by gorgeous apparel that the heretics wins proselytes, it is by zealous preaching, apostolic humility, by austerity, by seeming it is true, but by seeming holiness."[92] He claimed that the holiness of the Albigenses was counterfeit and needed to be stopped. The Albigenses were known for their extensive knowledge of the Scriptures and they also refused the teachings of Rome. At the Colloquy of Montreal in 1207 A.D. Dominic, as moderator of the Roman Catholic priesthood, openly debated the leader of the Albigenses. Dominic was clearly defeated in this debate. "Guzman was humiliated by his failure . . .

---

[91] *Leviathan*, Thomas Hobbes 1691
[92] http://www.christianity-guide.com/christianity/dominic_de_guzman.htm

Speaking on behalf of Christ, Guzman promised slavery and death" to his opponents.[93] To carry out his threats Dominic would eventually form the Order of the Dominicans which became the chief instrument of Rome's inquisition. Two years later, Pope Innocent III ordered the crusade against the Albigenses where tens of thousands lost their lives.

By 1233 A.D., Pope Gregory IX would establish the Inquisition as official Church doctrine and the next 600 years would be full of bloodshed against Bible believers. The popes began to outlaw the translation, possession and reading of the Bible. John Dowling estimated in 1845 that 50 million people lost their lives to Rome for their Biblical Christian beliefs.[94]

The first Bible translated into the English language was attributed to John Wycliffe. By approximately the year 1384, he translated from Latin into Middle English so that the people could adequately read the Scriptures. Because England was primarily Roman Catholic, many of Wycliffe's followers were put to death by the Church of Rome. Most were burned and if copies of Wycliffe's translation were found on them, they were tied to their necks and burned along with them. The Roman Catholic Church despised Wycliffe with such ferocity that in 1428 they actually exhumed his corpse, smashed it to pieces and then burned the bone fragments *again!*

The main method for the Roman Catholic Church to differentiate between a "heretic" and a faithful follower of their own Church was in the Roman Catholic doctrine of transubstantiation; where they teach that the wafer of bread consecrated by a priest is *the true body and divinity of Jesus Christ.*

True Bible believing Christians would deny this false doctrine and therefore when the wafer was held in front of their faces and they were forced to make a choice, they would not accept the teaching of Rome and would lose their lives.

---

[93] *Who's Who in the Cathar War: Dominic Guzman,* James McDonald www.cathar.info -*A Lamp in the Dark*

[94] *The History of Romanism,* John Dowling, 1845, page 541

The doctrine of transubstantiation was decreed by Pope Innocent III in 1215 A.D.[95] This doctrine is probably *the* strongest bondage to the Roman Catholic Church which keeps its followers from straying. This doctrine states that the wafer of bread and the wine are mysteriously transformed into the *literal* flesh and *literal* blood of Christ by the clergy member who consecrates the host.[96] "Hostia" in Latin means "victim." It is worshiped as though it is really Jesus Christ. This doctrine is the *core* of the "Sacrifice of the Mass" and many people believe that if they do not eat this bread and drink this wine each week at Mass, then they are committing a "mortal sin," which is punishable by an eternity in Hell. Roman Catholic Canon Law states, "If any one shall deny that the body and blood, together with the souls an divinity of our Lord Jesus Christ, and therefore entire Christ, are truly, really, and substantially contained in the sacrament of the most Holy Eucharist; and shall say that He is only in it as a sign, or in a figure, let him be accursed."[97] Accursed means to be damned to Hell for all of eternity.

In the Book of Revelation, John is told about the *Church of Thyatira* which historically became the papal Church. This signifies the beginnings of organized Roman Catholicism and began around 500 A.D. until the present time. Thyatira comes from the two words meaning "sacrifice" and "continual." The Church of Rome denies the finished work of Christ but believes in *a continual sacrifice* which is performed at each and every Mass celebration every day all over the world. They offer up the victim, "the host" as the "Sacrifice of the Mass." We need not "sacrifice" Jesus again and again on altar after altar as is done in the Roman Catholic Churches across the world because it is believed to gain them forgiveness of sins. Our sin debt was paid in *full* through the Sacrifice of Jesus *once and for all* the first time at Calvary. **Hebrews 10:11 says, "And every Priest stands daily Ministering and offering oftentimes the same Sacrifices, *which can never take away sins* (my italics)." Hebrews 9:24-26 says, "For Christ is not entered into the Holy Places made with hands . . . but to Heaven itself, now to appear in the Presence of God for us: Nor yet that He should offer Himself often, as the High Priest enters into the Holy Place every year with the blood of others** (speaking of the

---

95   *The Evangelist,* December 2006 edition, page 11
96   *Catechism of the Catholic Church,* Second Edition, 1997, paragraph 1376
97   Roman Catholic Code of Canon Law Council of Trent Canon I

blood of the sacrificial animals, used to represent the blood which Jesus would shed for us)**; For then must He often have suffered since the foundation of the world: but now once in the end of the world has He appeared to put away sin by the Sacrifice of Himself."** Then **Hebrews 10:10** says, **". . . we are sanctified through the Offering of the Body of Jesus Christ** *once for all* (my italics).**" "Once for all"** means that the sacrifice does not need repeating.

Roman Catholics may argue that they are not "re-sacrificing" Jesus at the Mass, but this is not true according to the Roman Catholic Church. The very *heart* of the Roman Catholic Mass is the "Sacrifice of the Mass," which is called the Eucharist.[98] It is also called an "unbloody sacrifice" in the *Catholic Encyclopedia* and the purpose of this sacrifice is for the remission of sins.[99] Let us look again at **Hebrews 9:22** where it states, **". . . and without the shedding of blood is no remission of sin . . ."** This means that if there is no blood shed then the sacrifice cannot take away sins; so an "unbloody sacrifice," as used in the Roman Catholic sacrament of the Eucharist, would be completely *useless*. The Council of Trent in 1562 stated that the sacrifice of Christ and the sacrifice of the Eucharist are *one single sacrifice* and are one in the same: It said, "The victim is one and the same: the same now offers through the ministry of priests, who then offered himself on the cross; only the manner of offering is different . . . And since in this divine sacrifice which is celebrated in the Mass, the same Christ who offered himself once in a bloody manner on the altar of the cross is contained and offered in an unbloody manner . . . this sacrifice is truly propitiatory."[100] Basically, this means that at the Mass, Jesus Christ offers Himself by the hands of a priest as a true and real sacrificial offering to gain favor with or appease (propitiate[101]) God. The clergy member officiating the mass actually says, "Pray, brethren, that our sacrifice may be acceptable to God, the almighty Father." The congregation responds by saying, "May the Lord accept the sacrifice at your hands for the praise and glory of his name, for our good, and the good of all his Church." This can only mean that this is a fresh sacrifice to God each and every time it is performed. Please read the

---

[98] *Catechism of the Catholic Church,* Second edition, 1997, paragraph 1330
[99] http://www.newadvent.org/cathen/10006a.htm
[100] http://www.usccb.org/catechism/text/pt2sect2chpt1art3.htm
[101] http://www.merriam-webster.com/dictionary/propitiate

next Scripture carefully. It is found in **Hebrews 6:6** and says, **"If they should fall away, to renew them again unto Repentance; seeing they crucify to themselves the Son of God afresh, and put *Him* to an open shame."** Most Catholics do not realize that the sacrifice of the Eucharist is *repeating* the crucifixion of Jesus and thereby putting **"Him to an open shame."**

The Reformation of the 1500's was greatly influenced because of brave soldiers of the Cross such as John Wycliffe, who was referred to as "The Morning Star of the Protestant Reformation." One noted follower was Jan Huss, a Bohemian Reformer who was burned at the stake in 1415 for denying the Roman Catholic doctrine of papal infallibility and for acknowledging the authority of the Bible. Before he died, Huss claimed that God had given him a promise. The name "Huss" means "goose" in the Czech language, and the Lord had told him, "They will silence the goose, but in 100 years, I will raise a swan from your ashes that no one will be able to silence."[102] A century later in 1517, inspired partly by the sermons from Jan Huss, Martin Luther, a Catholic priest, nailed his 95 Thesis to the door of the Wittenberg Church in Germany on October 31st. This brave act and the circulation of the material Luther had nailed to the Church door sparked the Reformation where many people left the strong arm of the Roman Catholic Church.

Those who opposed the papacy were deemed as "Protestants" by the pope of Rome because they were protesting against the teachings of the Roman Catholic Church. This is why it became known as "The Protestant Reformation." Many of the countries in Western Europe became Protestant and of the countries of Western Europe, only two, Italy and Spain, remained with the pope. Most of the reformers began as Catholic priests who did not agree with the erroneous doctrines of Rome and could see that the teachings of the Roman Catholic Church were contrary to the Word of God. Some examples are John Wycliffe, William Tyndale, Jan Huss, John Knox, Ulrich Zwingli and, of course, Martin Luther. The Bible was the weapon of choice used by the Reformers. It says specifically inside of its pages **"For the Word of God is quick, and powerful, and sharper than any two-edged sword . . . and is**

---

[102] *Jan Huss: The Goose of Bohemia*, William P. Farley

a discerner of the thoughts and intents of the heart (Hebrews 4:12)." The *New Advent Catholic Encyclopedia* online, under the term "Protestantism" states, "The supremacy of the Bible as source of faith is unhistorical, ill logical, fatal to the virtue of faith, and destructive of unity." This is what Roman Catholicism, led by the pope, thought about Bible supremacy! And of course, the Reformation was opposed by a *counter reformation* led by Ignatius Loyola who created the "Society of Jesus," known as the Jesuit Order, in 1540. This military order, directed by the Jesuit General, was the secret army of Rome in carrying out the famous inquisitions which killed millions of Bible believers.

The original Bible manuscripts were written in Hebrew and Greek and had been preserved for all generations just as God had promised us in **Psalms 12:6-7** where it says, **"The words of the LORD are pure words: as silver tried in a furnace of earth, purified seven times. You shall keep them, O LORD, You shall preserve them from this generation forever."** One of the goals of the Jesuits was to deface the true Bible, which they maliciously vowed to do. The Jesuits said, "Then the Bible, that serpent which, with head erect and eyes flashing fire, threatens us with its venom whilst it trails along the ground, shall be changed again into a rod as soon as we are able to seize it; For you know but too well that, for three centuries past, this cruel asp has left us no repose; you well know with what folds it entwines us, and with what fangs it gnaws us."[103]

They needed to first claim the Greek and Hebrew texts were corrupted and could not be trusted; and second, to claim that the *Latin Vulgate* was the superior text and inspired of the Holy Spirit. They also claimed that the Bible is too difficult to understand so one must trust in Roman Catholic Church tradition and the infallible pope to interpret it. As a result, they formed the *Douay Rheims Bible* based on the *Latin Vulgate*. On the other hand, the *Textus Receptus* was based on Erasmus' translation into Greek and Latin. Erasmus corrected the many corruptions by the Church of Rome in the *Latin Vulgate* before he translated the Scriptures into Greek. There will be more on Erasmus' contributions in the following paragraphs.

---

[103] *The Jesuit Conspiracy: The Secret Plan of the Order*, Abate Leone, Chapman and Hall, 1848, page 98

In 1440, Johan Gutenberg invented the moveable type which made production of Bibles much more accessible among the people. Prior to this method of printing, a single Bible copied by a scribe would take roughly 10 months to complete. In 1455, Gutenberg published the now famous *Gutenberg Bible* along with 200 copies in a single year. Needless to say, this was a major game changer! Unfortunately, Gutenberg's first Bible was based on the *Latin Vulgate* originally translated by Jerome supposedly in the fourth century and Jerome's translation was a wrong interpretation leaving out important portions of God's Word. It was based on the *Codex Vaticanus*, called so because it belongs to the Vatican Library and was proven to be a forgery. It leaves out over 400 words and over 700 sentences in the Gospels alone. Although it is claimed to have been written in the fourth century, most experts and scholars agree that it was most certainly written in the 15th century. *Codex Sinaiticus*, supposed scrolls found in a waste bin in a monastery, has over 14,000 revisions and is said to be the most revised manuscript in history. This proves that it is also a forgery accomplished by Constantine Von Tischendorff, an alleged Protestant from Germany who was awfully close to the pope and other Jesuit advisers in the Vatican. Of course the Jesuits like to use the many thousands of revisions and the *Codex Sinaiticus* as proof that the Bible is not inspired but most true Christians would not agree with the *Codex Sinaiticus* or the *Codex Vaticanus*. The *King James Bible*, accepted by true Christians, is derived from the *Textus Receptus* which completely lines up with the *Dead Sea Scrolls* discovered in 1946-56 in Israel. These scrolls were original preserved Scripture found stored in jars and written on parchment, papyrus and bronze which some dated back to before Jesus was born![104]

The city of Constantinople, built by Constantine, was originally built to replace Rome as the capital empire. But after Constantine's death, the Roman Empire was divided into the East and West divisions. While the West used Latin as their earlier form of Scripture, the East continued to use the Greek language. This eventually became known as the Byzantine Empire. Then in 1453, the Ottoman Empire led by the Islamic Sultan, Mohammed II, conquered Constantinople. As a result, many of the Byzantine scholars fled to the West bringing with them thousands of

---

[104] http://en.wikipedia.org/wiki/Dead_Sea_scrolls

manuscripts written in Greek. The Greek language began being taught in the universities in Europe. Erasmus was taught by some of these Greek scholars and he was instrumental in the Reformation as well, when he translated the first Greek New Testament as a single edition. He wrote a side by side translation with Latin on one side and Greek on the other side, both on the same page. This introduction into the Western world opened up a whole new understanding of the Bible. He appropriately corrected the translation corruptions with the *Latin Vulgate* after he translated into Greek. One example is that the Church of Rome had translated "repentance" into "penance" which changed the meaning of the text. Penance being a work instructed by a Roman Catholic priest after he has absolved someone of his or her sins in the Catholic sacrament of reconciliation; while "repentance" means turning away from sin and toward God's will.

Armed with Erasmus' Greek Bible translation, Martin Luther would translate the New Testament into German in 1522. From there William Tyndale translated from Greek to give us our English Bible. In a dinner conversation with a Roman Catholic priest where Tyndale kept referring to God's Word as authority, the priest stated, "We would be better to be without God's Law than the pope's law." Tyndale replied, "I defy the pope and all his laws, if God spare my life ere these many years, I will cause a boy that driveth the plow to know more of the Scriptures than thou dost." It became his life's work to create a Bible which the common people could read. He was hated and hunted by Rome and was finally strangled and burned at the stake in Belgium. But before Tyndale died, he spoke in a loud voice saying, "God! Open the King of England's eyes!" Six months later, King Henry ordered the Bible to be translated into English using the New Testament translation that William Tyndale had created. Previously the Roman Catholic Church had forbidden the common man to read the Bible, but now it was becoming the most widely read book around! This caused more hatred and bloodshed because the hierarchy of the Roman Catholic Church doesn't believe the common man can appropriately interpret the Scriptures for themselves. In *St. Josephs Annotated Catechism*, it says, ". . . the sacred text must be *rightly* understood, which is the role of the professional exegetes under the guidance of the Church . . ."[105] The Bible was even labeled a forbidden book to laymen and placed on the index of forbidden books by the Council of Toledo in A.D. 1229.[106]

England's King Henry VIII petitioned the pope of Rome for an annulment of his marriage to Anne Boleyn when she had not produced him a son as an heir. His chancellor was Sir Thomas More and both hated William Tyndale for his stand against Roman Catholic doctrine. The term "red tape" was derived from King Henry because of the many dozens of red seals used to petition the pope for an annulment, which were all denied. He eventually broke from the Church of Rome and had Thomas More beheaded as a traitor. He set himself up as the head of England's Church which came to be known as the Anglican Church and in some countries today is known as the Episcopal Church. The Anglican Church has the same seven sacraments as the Roman Catholic Church, as well as, the majority believe in the doctrine of transubstantiation.

Because Tyndale was able to translate much of the Old Testament from Hebrew to English before his imprisonment and death, it was his material that became the basis for which King Henry VIII used to commission *The Great Bible* of 1539. It was also used in 1557 for the *Geneva Bible*, which is well known today as "The Bible of the Reformation." Modern scholars believe that based on computer statistics, 83% of the *King James Version* of 1611 was based on Tyndale's English translation. Tyndale had managed to translate the entire New Testament and a portion of the Old Testament before his death. It was Miles Coverdale, a great friend of Tyndale, who completed the Old Testament translation from Hebrew to English after Tyndale's imprisonment and then death in 1536. He created the *Coverdale Bible* of 1535. This was the first complete Bible with both the Old and New Testaments printed in the English language. Then a follower of William Tyndale, John Rogers, under the pseudonym of Thomas Matthews, took both Tyndale and Coverdale's translations and created *The Matthews Bible* of 1537 which was the first complete Bible to be printed in England. Before that, Tyndale's New Testament was only printed in Germany and

---

[105] *St. Josephs Annotated Catechism*, Rev. Anthony Schraner, Catholic Book Publishing Co., New York, 1981, page 20 (italics in original)
[106] *The Evangelist*, December 2006 edition, page 11

Coverdale's in Switzerland. Thomas Cromwell was asked by Henry VIII to commission a scholar to create *The Great Bible* for the English Church and Miles Coverdale worked on that project as well. This Bible is also known as *The Cromwell Bible* of 1539. These huge Bibles were put in all of the Churches in England and sometimes called "the chained Bible" because of the fact that they were chained to the pulpit.

The Roman Catholic Church was very displeased with the various Bible translations, as well as, the fact that England had cast off the authority of the pope. The Bible in the common language openly disputed against the doctrinal teachings of Rome. In 1547, Henry VIII died and his nine year old son, Edward VI, was put on the throne of England. King Edward believed in the cause of the Reformers and also believed the Roman Catholic Church along with the pope to be corrupt and contrary to the Word of God. For a time, England would become a firm Protestant nation. At only 11 years old, King Edward wrote, "The pope is the true son of the Devil, a bad man, an Antichrist, an abominable tyrant."[107]

In February 1553, at the age of only 15 years old, Edward died. Many speculate he was slowly poisoned to death, mostly because of the drawn out illness and the symptoms he displayed before he died.[108] But before his death, when his sickness was seen as terminal, he and his council drew up a "Devise for the Succession," attempting to prevent the country from being returned to Roman Catholicism. Edward named his cousin, Lady Jane Grey, as his heir and excluded his half-sisters, Mary and Elizabeth. However, this was disputed following Edward's death and within 9 days, Jane was deposed by Edward's Roman Catholic sister, Mary. Queen Mary I reversed Edward's Protestant reforms and once again came into communion with the Roman Catholic Church using the instrument of Royal Supremacy. She became known as "Bloody Mary" because of the many Protestants she had put to death as "heretics" of the Roman Catholic Church. She ordered all of the copies of the Bible in English to be burned.[109] Mary also ordered anyone who was translating

---

[107] King Edward VI, as cited by David J.B. Trim, in "Reformation and Counter Reformation" Liberty Magazine, May/June 2009
[108] http://englishmonarchs.co.uk/tudor_6.htm
[109] *The History and the Impact of the Geneva Bible*, Gary DeMar

or reading the Bible to be burned as well. She burned John Rogers who had published *The Matthews Bible*. Some 800 English scholars fled the country to avoid Mary's bloody outrage and many ended up in Geneva, Switzerland under the protection of John Calvin and other Reformers.

By using the original Hebrew and Greek and much of Tyndale's translation and without the constraints of Rome and the crown of England, such scholars as John Knox and Miles Coverdale created *The Geneva New Testament* of 1557. When Mary I died in 1558, her half-sister Elizabeth I succeeded her. Elizabeth I installed the Elizabethan Religious Settlement of 1559 where she re-established the Church of England's independence from Roman Catholicism. Of course, Pope Pius V responded with The Papal bull *Regnans in Excelsis*, issued on 25 February 1570, declaring, "Elizabeth, the pretended Queen of England and the 'servant of crime' to be a heretic, released all of her subjects from any allegiance to her, and excommunicated any who obeyed her orders."[110] By 1560, a complete version of the *Geneva Bible* was published and dedicated to the new Queen of England, Elizabeth I. This is the same Bible brought over to the New World by the Pilgrims.

This is a brief history of the timeline of how the Bible got into the hands of the people. Many people lost their lives to afford us the privilege of reading God's Word so it should certainly not be taken for granted! Of course, since this time the Bible has been re-published almost too many times to count. In order for someone to publish something that has previously been published, they must change a certain percentage of the material. This has caused many translations of the Bible and even worse, some paraphrase Bibles to be put on the market.

Jesuit trained, John Henry took over Thomas Nelson Publishing, the largest publishing conglomerate of Bibles.[111] He openly admits an interview in 2001 that he aspired to go from a blue-collar worker to an extremely successful business person because he was trained at a Jesuit University and he gave the Jesuit Order all of the credit for his success. This is so detrimental because the Jesuits of the Roman Catholic Church have said, "Then the Bible, that serpent which, with head erect and eyes

---

[110] http://en.wikipedia.org/wiki/Elizabethan_Religious_Settlement
[111] *Tares Among the Wheat* DVD, Adullam Film Productions, 2012: 2:48

flashing fire, threatens us with its venom whilst it trails along the ground, *shall be changed again into a rod as soon as we are able to seize it*; For you know but too well that, for three centuries past, this cruel asp has left us no repose; you well know with what folds it entwines us, and with what fangs it gnaws us (my italics)."[112] John Henry even goes so far as to say that he was inspired by demons and devils! In 2011, John Henry's company sold Thomas Nelson Publishing to Rupert Murdoch, owner of Fox News. Murdoch is a member of the Knights of St. Gregory, knighted by the pope of Rome. Thomas Nelson Publishing now publishes the *New King James Version Bible*. And through Zondervan Publishing, he publishes the *New International Version*. Murdoch also owns Harper Collins publishing house, which puts out Anton LeVay's *Satanic Bible* for the Church of Satan.

Roman Catholic Rupert Murdoch's ownership over Harper Collins Publishing makes it possible for the Roman Catholic Church to have the legal copyright to all newer Bible versions! It is a little known fact that all the new Bible versions (*New International Version, New American Standard Version*, etc.) are based not on the original manuscript from which the *King James Version* was derived, the *Textus Receptus*, but on the two so-called "ancient" manuscripts found in the custody of the Roman Catholic Church: The *Codex Sinaiticus* and the *Codex Vaticanus*. As mentioned earlier, proof that the *Codex Sinaiticus* is a forgery comes in many forms, as well as, has been significantly altered in many places. James Bentley writes in his book, *Secrets of Mount Sinai* that there are "14,800 such corrections made by nine separate correctors."[113]

John Wylie said, "There are two institutions in special to which the Jesuits will lay siege. These are the press and the pulpit, the press of Great Britain is already manipulated by them to an extent of which the public but little dream. The whole English press of the world is supervised, and the word is passed around how writers, speakers, and causes are to be handled and applause or condemnation dealt out just as it may accord

---

[112] *The Jesuit Conspiracy: The Secret Plan of the Order*, Abate Leone, Chapman and Hall, 1848, page 98
[113] *Secrets of Mount Sinai*, James Bentley, page 118

with the interests and wishes of Rome."[114] With the manipulation of the many Bible translations and the changing of the method of preaching using the Seeker Sensitive Church movements of today, tremendous damage is being done to true Christianity. This has been done through careful influence of the Jesuits of the Roman Catholic Church, under the guidance of Satan himself. Please remember that the Jesuits are just pawns in the hands of Satan. He is the puppet master using them to accomplish the destruction of God's Word, which will set men free!

---

[114] *The Jesuits: Their Morals, Maxims and Plots against Kings, Nations and Churches.* By J. A. Wylie Pages 93 - 94.

IS HISTORY REPEATING ITSELF?

From Malachi, the last prophet of the Old Testament, until the time of Christ was approximately 400 years. This time span is sometimes referred to as the "silent" years, but there were plenty of pertinent historical events which took place during this era. For example, when the Old Testament period closed, Judea was still under Persian dominance. If we look again at the Book of Daniel, Persia was the empire which defeated the Babylonians in 538 B.C. This nation was represented by the breastplate of silver on Nebuchadnezzar's statue. But in studying the statue, we know that the Greek and Roman Empires had yet to be established. As a result of the Persian victory over Babylon, the Jews were liberated from captivity. They were able to return home to Jerusalem and rebuild their temple. Unfortunately, the people became apathetic in their commitment to God once again. The Persians were the governing political power which continued until the Greek period beginning in 332 B.C. under Alexander the Great who became the dominating world power at that time. When Alexander died at the age of just 32 years old, his kingdom was divided into four parts: Egypt, Syria, Thrace and Greece.

These four kingdoms began warring against one another. Antiochus III of Syria gave his daughter, 11 year old Cleopatra, to Egypt's Ptolemy V in marriage with the intentions of her acting as a spy for Syria. But ultimately, she sided with her Egyptian husband and defeated her father's plans by inviting the protection of the Romans **(Daniel 11:17)**. Syria did conquer Egypt but then Rome stepped in and forced them to surrender **(Daniel 11:14)**. Then Antiochus attacked Asia Minor and Greece, but the Roman General Lucius Scipio defeated him **(Daniel 11:18)**. Eventually Rome took control of the city of Jerusalem in 63 B.C. just as Daniel's interpretation of the statue revealed. However, they allowed the temple worship to continue in Jerusalem. Judea and Jerusalem were made tributaries to the Romans, thus ending the independence for the Jews which they experienced while under the control of the Persian Empire. A yearly tribute had to be paid to the Romans, which most of the Jews absolutely detested.

Herod was king of Judah when Jesus was born and, being a brutal and cruel man, he ordered the murder of the children of Bethlehem in an attempt to destroy the "King of the Jews." Jesus' birth in Bethlehem and life in Nazareth were not simply by chance. His coming was ordained by God and was achieved when all of the preparations had been made. The Apostle Paul declares in **Galatians 4: 4, 5, "But when the fullness of the time was come, God sent forth His Son . . . to redeem them who were under the Law . . ."** *The world conditions were precisely ready for God's supreme revelation in history!* The social, economic, moral, religious, and other factors had all converged to provide the proper setting for the manifestation of the Son of God. The study of world conditions at the time of the birth of Christ has some practical value, which lies in the discovery of the modern conditions which parallel the return of Christ. Please read the next several paragraphs carefully and look at the conditions of today in comparison to the time when Jesus came to Earth the first time as a Redeemer for mankind.

The *political preparation* was one such condition. The known world had been unified under Caesar's power and that entire area was under Roman domination. Frontiers between all of the countries were open, resulting in good roads and travel. Transportation on the high seas was also possible. These were some of the factors involved in the political preparation that would enhance the spread of the Gospel once Jesus did come. The language of the people was another factor relating to the political preparation and world unity at the time when Jesus came. There was no language barrier because most all of the people spoke Greek. Each province had its own tongue or dialect, but Greek was the common language. Remember, the New Testament was written in Greek.

Not only in the fullness of time was the political preparation accomplished, but also the *economic preparation*. Great luxury abounded on one hand, while unrest and poverty on the other. Two out of every three people on the streets of Rome were slaves, considered no more than property of the state. Many of them rebelled and desired to go free. The majority of the people lived under much difficulty and economic depression. So many were at their wits end and desperately needed to be rescued, so the coming of Christ into human history was a much anticipated event for some. There was a breakdown of all human resources, and many were prepared to listen to Christ to find hope and Eternal Life. They were weary from being in the bondage of slavery to the Roman Empire.

The world was also ready in the *moral preparation*, because the Roman world had sunk to the state of utter moral hopelessness. It would take the Spirit of Christ to change the moral fiber of men and nations. This is also true in today's world. The moral fibers of society are fast degenerating and wickedness is becoming greater and greater. **2 Timothy 3:13** says, **"But evil men and seducers shall wax worse and worse, deceiving, and being deceived."** The hearts of many people long for the return of Christ and for the establishment of the Kingdom of God and the Millennial Reign of Jesus Christ.

The *religious preparation* was also important when Jesus came the first time. The old gods of Rome were meaningless. There were mystery religions and idols of various kinds. Also, the worship of Caesar, the emperor himself, was given divine honors. But all of these had failed and the hearts of the people were spiritually hungry. The Jews themselves had been looking for centuries for their Messiah. The great mass of their literature during the period between the Old Testament and New Testament was full of the hope of the coming Messiah. When John the Baptist began to preach and his voice rang out from the wilderness, the people began to look for the Man that John the Baptist was introducing. Certainly the fullness of time had come! "The Redeemer came in a time ordained by God; a time that had been prepared in many ways; and a time needing the Redeemer."[115]

It is often said that "history repeats itself." The Father of Communism, Karl Marx, even said, *"History repeats itself, first as tragedy, second as farce."* The word "farce" meaning a travesty or a mockery. It has also been said that there is a cycle of "the rise of a civilization": Productivity > Territorial Expansion > Economic collapse > Fall of civilization > and then a repeat of the same cycle.

Satan generally has two weapons: violence and flattery. While the Roman Empire was in power during the first advent of Jesus, they most certainly used violence to intimidate, subdue their victims and gain control. Once Jesus died on the Cross and was raised from the dead, He gave His Disciples "the Great Commission" immediately before He ascended into Heaven to go out and preach the Gospel to the world **(Mark 16:15)**. The Early Church began fulfilling this commission after they were baptized in the Holy Spirit on the Day of Pentecost **(Acts 2:4)**. Because of the persecution of the Romans and the religious Jews, the followers of Jesus were dispersed to different areas where they preached **"Jesus Christ and Him crucified (1 Corinthians 2:2)."** Rome continued in power and then, of course, the Roman Emperor Constantine issued the Edict of Milan in 313 A.D. making Rome neutral in regards to worship and sets himself up as the leader of this new pagan universal Church. Before this time, the Roman Empire was just a controlling government force, but adding religion to the government made them the spiritual and temporal power on Earth. The Roman Catholic Church gained tremendous wealth and power and subordinated all of the kings of the Earth and all of the people with her religious system. This time, referred to as the "Dark Ages" kept the Word of God from the people and the crusades, massacres and inquisitions killed millions upon millions of Christians, Jews and others who would not bow down to the pope of Rome. But God used men such as Martin Luther to spark the Reformation and bring the Light of Jesus Christ back into the world again. The Counter Reformation led by Ignatius Loyola and the Jesuit Order then rose to power under the approval of Pope Paul III and

---

[115] *Expositor's Study Bible*, 2005, Jimmy Swaggart *Between the Testaments,* pages 1642-1644

attempted to gain back the spiritual and temporal power for the papacy which was slowly diminishing as people were leaving the Roman Catholic Church. The people, who were labeled as "Protestants," grew weary and tired of persecution. They set out to find a new land where they could be free from persecution and from the threat of the Roman Catholic Inquisitions.

Unfortunately the Jesuits followed in disguise and planted Roman Catholics posing as Protestants all over the New World to infiltrate and destroy everything the Protestants were building. The United States became a nation in 1776, the same year that Jesuit Adam Weishaupt began the Order of the Illuminati where the goals were identical to that of the Jesuit Order. In 1790, the city of Rome, Maryland became our nation's capital and was renamed "Washington D.C." by Jesuit trained Daniel Carroll. In 1882, the Knights of Columbus, an American Catholic fraternity, came into existence to be the strong arm of the pope here in America. Their motto is "MAC," which means "Make America Catholic." In the late 1800's and early 1900's, there was a push for a unified world government by Jesuit trained Cecil Rhodes. Then in the early 1900's the Azusa Street Revival began and ignited the fire of the Holy Spirit all over the world! Satan counteracted this move with the Jesuit created New Age Movement, Humanistic Psychology, and the new social gospel which has been implemented in almost all mainline denominations, as well as Evangelical Churches in the form of Seeker Sensitive Churches, Purpose Driven Churches and Emerging Churches.

Shortly after, the Jesuits set up the Federal Reserve Bank in 1913 as a money machine to fund their various wars and activities. This gave them great power in the United States and consequently, the government, judicial system, media, and educational systems are presently almost completely run by the Jesuits. In 1962, the Vatican II Council was assembled beginning the Ecumenical Movement which was then reinforced in 1986 when Pope John Paul summoned 12 major religions to join in prayer to a common "god." Also in 1994, the "Evangelicals and Catholics Together: The Christian Mission in the Third Millennium" was signed. This was a blatant reversal of the Reformation and a push for religious unity, which is not possible for true Bible believing born again Christians to join. This united religious system is the one world religion which will be under the leadership of Antichrist's false prophet spoken of in the Book of Revelation **(Revelation 13:11-18)**.

Now, two centuries after the founding of this great nation of America, the Jesuits, are putting their final touches on the internal annihilation of the United States as they prepare for another inquisition which will give them total and complete power over America and the entire temporal world, a plan which has really been in the making since the Tower of Babel.

Now, let me revert back to the statement about Satan using "violence" and also" flattery" as his primary weapons to obtain power. We know that Rome used extreme violence throughout the centuries to become wealthy and powerful. No doubt, it seemingly worked to gain control, but it did not stop the Gospel from going forth because it was a divine ordinance from God Almighty that it be preached to every corner of the Earth before the return of Jesus Christ. God has always kept a remnant who believes His Word and can see through the deceptions of Satan. We can certainly see how Rome turned over a new leaf beginning in 1962 and continuing until this present hour. Sadly, the motives have not changed; she still desires world domination and complete control over the people of this Earth. The means by which she will attempt to attain it have only changed: *from violence to flattery.*

Remember **Daniel 11:21** where it stated, **"And in his estate shall stand up a vile person, to whom they shall not give honour of the kingdom: but he shall come in peaceably, and obtain the kingdom by flatteries."** This was speaking of a type of the Antichrist, Antiochus Epiphanies. Also, in **Revelation 13:11**, speaking of the false prophet, it says, **"And I beheld another beast coming up out of the earth; and he had two horns like a lamb, and he spoke as a dragon."** The connotation as **"a lamb"** denotes him as a meek and humble creature, but as one can see in the Scripture, it says that **"he spoke as a dragon."** The only time the word **"dragon"** is mentioned in Scripture is when it is referring to evil and more specifically, Satan in many instances.

God warns us in **1 Thessalonians 5:3**, where it says, **"For when they shall say, Peace and safety, then sudden destruction comes**

upon them, as travail upon a woman with child; and they shall not escape." There is a call for world peace and unity by many political and religious leaders of the world today. While religious unity may *sound* wonderful, it will never materialize here on this sin-ridden Earth until Jesus, the **"Prince of Peace (Isaiah 9:6),"** comes back to rule and reign here. No man or woman can usher in a true lasting time of peace except Jesus Christ! An interesting note is that on the day when Jesus was born in Bethlehem, far away in Rome, the war Gates of Janus were closed which signified peace throughout the world. They remained that way the entire time Jesus was present here on Earth! This was not done purposefully by Roman Emperor Augustus because he had no way of knowing that the world's Saviour had been born in a tiny stable in Bethlehem; but God knew it and therefore brought about a time of peace.

From all accounts, the conditions today are parallel to the conditions of the first time Jesus came, meaning that our world is ripe for His second coming. Rome is still secretly in power, with the majority of the known world completely deceived by her intentions. History has been rewritten to cover up her gory past and most, including many Christians, have been fooled by the false unity and peace that the Roman Catholic Church is marketing. People seemed to have forgotten the millions upon *millions* who have lost their lives in the awful inquisitions because they would not accept the authority of the Roman Catholic Church. People may or may not realize that the Roman Catholic Church claims to be the *one and only true Church* and that they assert that there is absolutely no salvation outside of their sacramental system. People do not recognize that it is the Roman Catholic majority in our nation's Congress[116] who are tearing our great country down and selling the scraps to the highest bidder. Many brave men have spent their entire adult lives warning about the imminent threat of Rome, but they have been discredited, silenced and even killed. The next chapter will highlight the warnings of a few of these Godly men who were not afraid to stand as **"watchmen upon the walls (Isaiah 62:6)"** to warn the people that an enemy was in their midst.

---

[116] http://www.ncregister.com/daily-news/meet-the-catholics-in-congress

Chapter Eight

WARNING AFTER WARNING

Satan's plan is always to corrupt God's Word and defame God's promises. He needs the cooperation of mankind to do his work on Earth. He has certainly found that in the Roman Catholic Jesuit Order. Just to recap, this group of men was initially formed in the early 1500s to reverse the Reformation which began with Martin Luther. Because many were leaving the Roman Catholic Church, Ignatius Loyola approached Pope Paul III with his ideas to bring the Protestants back to "Mother Church." This religious system has claimed throughout the centuries to be the one and only true Church where there is no salvation outside of its sacramental structure. Pope Benedict XVI reasserted on July 10, 2007 that the Roman Catholic Church is the *one and only true Church* and that "Orthodox Churches are defective, as well as, that other Christian denominations are not true Churches."[117]

After the Reformation, the Council of Trent was formed which gave public anathemas to many Biblical doctrines including salvation by faith in Jesus Christ alone and the assurance of one's salvation. They deemed that anyone who believed these Biblical doctrines was condemned to Hell. The Council of Trent also pronounced anathemas upon anyone who did not believe in transubstantiation, which is the belief that the wafer of

---

[117] http://www.msnbc.msn.com/id/19692094/

bread is magically transformed into the true body and divinity of Jesus Christ. Along with the Council of Trent, the inquisitions were continued in even more horrendous ways. These two means combined with the formation of the Jesuit Order, which was their secret weapon, were used as scare tactics to bring people back into the Roman Catholic Church or kill those who would not comply.

Eventually, the Jesuits became so powerful that they were seen as a threat even to the papal throne. While the "Black Pope" and "White Pope" work together, you must remember that there is *an agenda*. If the "White Pope" is not cooperative or threatens to have more power than the "Black Pope," he is a *dead man*. Alexander Robinson, wrote in his book, *The Roman Catholic Church in Italy*, "The General of the Jesuits, the 'Black Pope,' is the real and only pope. The one who bears the title [the "White Pope"] is but a figurehead. It is the Jesuits' policy he pursues, their voice that speaks through him, their hand that guides him. When illustrating this fact to me, Count Campello, who was a great friend of the late Pope Pius IX, drew a circle and said, 'Within that circle, he [the "White Pope"] is free; if he crosses it, *he is a dead man*.'" [118]

Loyola and the Jesuits devised a plan which would give them the absolute power to govern the pope of Rome in all things spiritual and political. Then, once this was accomplished, they were to consolidate all religious and political power into the hands of the pope, who in turn is directed by the Jesuit General. Because of their wicked deeds and power hungry attitude, the Jesuit Order was suppressed in 1773 by Pope Clement XIV, who was then slowly poisoned to death by the Jesuits. When the third Jesuit General, Francesco Borgia stated, "We came in like lambs, and will rule like wolves. *We shall be expelled like dogs and return like eagles,*" he truly meant exactly what he said! When the Jesuits were reinstated by Pope Pius VII in 1814, the Jesuit General began his very quick climb to the top of the ranks. By 1836, Pope Gregory XVI issued a brief *resigning the papacy to the control of the Society of Jesus*. Their mission for power over the White Pope was now accomplished! Any pope who would attempt to remove the power of the Jesuit General would meet a very untimely death. One case and point was in 1978 when John Paul

---

[118] *The Roman Catholic Church in Italy*, Alexander Robertson, page 51

I was murdered just 33 days in office for his attempt to remove Jesuit General Pedro Arrupe.

Now that the plan to have control over the papal throne was successful, the Jesuits needed to make sure that their public figurehead, the White Pope, was respected as the spiritual and temporal head so that the Black Pope could rule behind the scenes through him. At the *First Vatican Council* held in 1870, Pope Pius IX, who by this time was already under the ruling thumb of the Jesuit General, was declared to be "infallible," as well as, any successive pope after him. What does the term "infallible" actually mean? Papal infallibility claims that the followers of the Roman Catholic Church are expected to believe that the pope is without error and that a person may not even question his final decisions on the subject of faith and morals. Infallibility means more than exemption from actual error; it means exemption from the *possibility* of error.[119] Now that the people of the Roman Catholic Church were brainwashed into believing that their leader was infallible, the Jesuit General could decree almost anything through the many papal bulls and encyclicals while the blinded sheep would simply accept it as the Word of Almighty God.

The biggest threat to the Vatican and the Jesuit General is the freedom and liberty of individuals and of nations and *especially* freedom of religion. It is in direct opposition to the Universal Temporal Power and Universal Spiritual Power desired by the pope of Rome and the Jesuit General. On March 4th, 1789, in the first amendment to the Constitution, it stated, "Congress shall make no law respecting an establishment of religion or prohibiting the free exercise thereof." In comparing the *Constitution of the United States of America* with the principles of the Church of Rome, Charles Chiniquy, who spent fifty years inside of the Roman Catholic Church before he departed, wrote:

1st The most sacred principle of the United States Constitution is the equality of every citizen before the law. But the fundamental principle of the Church of Rome is the denial of that equality.

---

[119] http://www.newadvent.org/cathen/07790a.htm

2nd Liberty of conscience is proclaimed by the United States, a most sacred principle which every citizen must uphold, even at the price of his blood. But liberty of conscience is declared by all the popes and councils of Rome, a most godless, unholy, and diabolical thing, which every good Catholic must abhor and destroy at any cost.

3rd The American Constitution assures the absolute independence of the civil from the ecclesiastical or church power; but the Church of Rome declares that such independence is an impiety and revolt against God.

4th The American Constitution leaves every man free to serve God according to the dictates of his conscience; but the Church of Rome declares that no man has ever had such a right, and that the Pope alone can know and say what man must believe and do.

5th The Constitution of the United States denies the right for anybody to punish any other for differing from him in religion; but the Church of Rome says that she has the right to punish with the confiscation of their goods, or the penalty of death, those who differ in faith from the pope.

6th The Constitution of the United States is based on the principle that the people are the primary source of all civil power. But hundreds of times, the Church of Rome has proclaimed that this principle is impious and heretical. She says that all government must rest upon the foundation of the Catholic faith; with the pope alone as the legitimate and infallible source and interpreter of the law.[120]

Charles Chiniquy was one of the many watchmen sent by God who was not afraid to expose the adversary within our country. Another such man was Justin Fulton who published a warning to the American people in his 1888 book titled, *Washington in the Lap of Rome*. He desperately pleads with American to wake up before it is too late, exposing the deep deception which the Roman Catholic Church, along with the Jesuits, have created in the country of America. The dedication in his book states: "to Americans who will aid in throttling Jesuitism, in uncoiling the serpent encircling the capital of the United States, and in taking Washington out of the lap of Rome; That a free Church and a free school in a free state, may make the great Republic the glory of the world: This book is dedicated, in prayer and hope."

---

[120] *Fifty Years in the Church of Rome,* Charles Chiniquy, Chick Publications, 1985 (abridged from the 1886 version), page 284

What Justin Fulton saw happening in America was so compelling that he could not resist but to warn the people of the impending destruction if this cunning serpent was not dealt with swiftly. Unfortunately, the American people have only become more apathetic and more tolerant of evil in our country. My belief, along with many others in the true blood bought Church, is that America will be judged for her sins. America has allowed abortion to be legalized and homosexuality to be accepted and promoted. It seems that every warning in the Bible regarding sin; America has not only tolerated it but has also allowed it to be mainstreamed into television, movies, as well as, the print media. God *despises* sin and He will not allow this country to stand if it continues to go into perdition. Fulton even warns, "In a few years Rome will become able to establish the Inquisition here unless a speedy change for the better comes over the spirit of our people."[121] He describes the cells and underground passages in the cellar of Georgetown University in Washington and cells with thick walls, some made of iron, in many of the Roman Catholic Churches which he fears will be used to torture people "if the Catholics become a considerable majority" in America.

Justin Fulton could clearly see how Rome had climbed to power in Washington mainly because men had forgotten country and God, and served evil for the sake of gain.[122] He also saw how the Jesuits had overtaken Washington by using deceptive means. One of their famous quotations says "all things to all men," meaning that they can play any part which includes siding with the enemy to further the agenda of the Jesuit Order. It was imperative that the Jesuits would stake their claim in politics. Early on, they planted their "tares" among the "wheat" in the political arena and we are seeing what the harvest is now producing. As a result, we are a weakened and poisoned nation steeped in idolatry and sin.

Fulton said, "The Constitution of the United States finds in the people the source of civil power. Rome proclaims this principle impious and heretical, and claims that all governments must rest upon the foundations of the Catholic faith, with the pope alone as the legitimate

---

[121] *Washington in the Lap of Rome*, Justin Fulton, Hard Press Publishing, 1888, pages 66-67

[122] *Washington in the Lap of Rome*, Justin Fulton, Hard Press Publishing, 1888, page 66

and infallible source and interpreter of the law. The Honorable Richard W. Thompson, late Secretary of the Navy, said, 'Nothing is plainer than that, if the principles of the Church of Rome prevail here, religious freedom is at an end. The two cannot exist together.'" He also reveals a statement made by the Roman Catholic Bishop Ryan speaking in Philadelphia, where he said, "We maintain that the Church of Rome is intolerant; that is, that she uses every means in her power to root out heresy. But her intolerance is the result of her infallibility. She alone has the right to be intolerant, because she alone has the truth. The Church tolerates heretics when she is obliged to do so; but she hates them with a deadly hatred, and uses all her power to annihilate them. If ever the Catholics should become a considerable majority, which in time will surely be the case, then will religious freedom in the Republic of the United States come to an end."[123] You see, "The Roman Catholic is to wield his vote for the purpose of securing Catholic ascendency in this country. They vote as servants of the pope, not as patriots."[124] The sleeping Americans need to know these alarming quotations!

In the hierarchy of the Roman Catholic Church, a "cardinal" has a high ranking position. According to Wikipedia, "A cardinal is a senior ecclesiastical official, an ecclesiastical prince, and usually an ordained bishop. The cardinals of the Roman Catholic Church are collectively known as the College of Cardinals." Their duties include attending important meetings at the College of Cardinals and making themselves available to the pope. Some lead diocese or archdiocese. The other main function is in the electing of a new pope when necessary. In *Washington in the Lap of Rome*, it states, "In the United States, the cardinal is the mouthpiece and servant of the Order."[125] And in the preface, it says, ". . . a private wire runs from the White House, in Washington, to the cardinal's palace, in Baltimore, and that every important question touching the interest of Romanism in America is placed before his eye, before it becomes a public act, it is true that the cardinal is a factor in politics." Then it states, "The actual ruler of this nation lives not in the

---

[123] *Washington in the Lap of Rome*, Justin Fulton, Hard Press Publishing, 1888, page 70
[124] *Washington in the Lap of Rome*, Justin Fulton, Hard Press Publishing, 1888, page 127
[125] *Washington in the Lap of Rome*, Justin Fulton, Hard Press Publishing, 1888, page 65

White House at Washington, but in the Palace Baltimore (referring to the cardinal in charge)."[126] As anyone can see, the cardinal is a very powerful individual and the Vatican makes sure that there are influential men appointed as heads of the areas they want to control. What Fulton was trying to get across is the unbelievable power and control the Roman Catholic Church has by means of their appointed cardinals. And, of course, the cardinals are under the constant control of the Jesuit General.

Look at this statement made by a Jesuit showing the election process of the President of the United States: "Now, listen to me a few moments and I will tell you what I know. Your president is elected by the conclave of cardinals at Rome, the same who elect the pope. Your people nominate the candidates. Our confidential agents select from the number, the one whom they believe to be the most favorable to the interests of the Church. His name, with those of the other candidates, is reported to the cardinals and the pope. When their decision is announced to the confidential friends of the pope and the cardinals in the United States, they send forth their orders through the priests; and the whole Roman Catholic vote is thrown for the candidate who is favored by the Church. *He, of course, is always elected.* Your parties are so equally divided on politics, that this Roman Catholic vote, which is cast on purely religious considerations, is always sufficient to turn the scale (my italics)."[127]

Of course, part of the game plan of the Black Pope and the White Pope, is to make America predominantly Roman Catholic. A country full of faithful Roman Catholics would secure their control using our voting process against us. Common sense tells us that the more Roman Catholics they have voting, then the more Roman Catholics will be in positions of power and ultimately the more control the Vatican, under the rule of the Jesuit General, will have over the United States. So how did the Roman Catholics become the majority enabling them to elect whomever they see fit to further the domination of the Vatican here in the United States? This certainly did not happen overnight and took careful scheming and patience.

---

[126] *Washington in the Lap of Rome*, Justin Fulton, Hard Press Publishing, 1888, page 25
[127] *The Crisis: Or, The Enemies of America Unmasked*, J. Wayne Laurens, G. D. Miller, 1855, page 13

As you will recall, the colonists had fled Europe to avoid the persecution of the Church of Rome and to create a safe haven for freedom of conscience and religion. These settlers felt that the pope of Rome, as a foreign ruler, should *not* be allowed to meddle in the politics or laws of America and they also suspected that Roman Catholic immigrants would continue to be loyal to the papacy instead of the new country. For example, in 1647 a Massachusetts statute was declared that every Roman Catholic priest was an "incendiary and disturber of the public peace and safety, and an enemy of . . . true Christian religion."[128] The Roman Catholic bishops were required to take an oath stating, "I will to the utmost of my power seek out and oppose schismatics, heretics and the enemies of our Sovereign Lord [the pope] and his successors." This oath was later removed by Jesuit Bishop John Carroll, as to calm the fears that the bishops were really puppets of the pope of Rome.

The five laws adopted by the British Parliament in 1774, called the "Intolerable Acts" by the American colonists, were used to create a deep resentment and rebellion in the hearts of the American people. These five laws were clearly inflammatory acts meant to provoke a radical response from the colonists. A war was inevitable and it was exactly what the pope needed to create sympathy for the Roman Catholic religion allowing it to flourish within the New World. You see, many Roman Catholic joined forces with the colonists against Britain. As one Jesuit General stated, "We have men for martyrdom if they be required." Fighting and dying in the American Revolution was a small price to pay for Rome's advantage in America. This caused the respect for Roman Catholics to grow and thus, an influx of Roman Catholic immigrants and Jesuits to be allowed into the new United States of America.

Jesuit John Carroll wrote in a report sent to Rome, "In 1776, American Independence was declared, and a revolution effected, not only in political affairs, but also in those relating to religion. For a while the thirteen provinces of North America rejected the yoke of England . . . Before this great event, the Catholic faith had penetrated two provinces only, Maryland and Pennsylvania. In all others the laws against Catholics were in force . . . (But) By the Declaration of Independence, every

---

[128] *Codeword Barbelon*, P.D. Stuart, Lux-Verbi Books, 2009, page 306

difficulty was removed . . . every political disqualification was done away."[129] There was careful calculating to create this war and invoke the American Colonists to anger, but the results were exactly what the Church of Rome wanted and needed to quietly slip their pagan ungodly religion in the back door and make it acceptable in America. The results have been long lasting as now they have been able to take control of our armed forces, our government, our media, our press, our schools, our hospitals and every other facet of our lives. Here is another example of the title of this book taken from **Matthew 13:25**, where it says, **"But while men slept, His enemy came and sowed tares among the wheat, and went his way."**

The Vatican has been increasing the Roman Catholic population through immigration, both legal and illegal. Cardinal Roger Mahony of Los Angeles has been a key player in lobbying for the continued influx of immigrants into the United States, even calling all priest to "defy the law" if the immigration bill is passed![130] Faithful Roman Catholics are forbidden by Church law to use any kind of birth control besides what they refer to as "natural family planning." Most who use this method will tell you that it is not very effective! What does this mean for the United States? Well, for example, Frosty Wooldridge writes, "Mexico will grow from its current 104 million people to well over 300 million in this century. If Mexicans can't find a better life in their home country in 2007—30, 40 to 50 million will stream over U.S. borders in the coming years." You do the math; 30-50 million Roman Catholic Mexican immigrants who do not use birth control could mean disastrous results for our country and its citizens in the form of over population, the economy and not to mention the Roman Catholic majority it gives the Church of Rome here in America!

Charles Chiniquy, wrote in the late 1800's, "Rome saw at once that the very existence of the United States was a formidable menace to her own life."[131] He also recognized that Rome first needed a Roman Catholic majority here in America, so they began to send immigrant families

---

[129] *Codeword Barbelon*, P.D. Stuart, Lux-Verbi Books, 2009, page 313

[130] http://www.npr.org/templates/story/story.php?storyId=5246128

[131] *Fifty Years in the Church of Rome*, Charles Chiniquy, Chick Publications, page 291

here from all over the world to settle in "the states." Here is a Jesuit quote from *Fifty Years in the Church of Rome*, "Silently and patiently, we must mass our Roman Catholics in the great cities of the United States, remembering that the vote of a poor journeyman, though he be covered with rags, has as much weight in the scale of powers as the millionaire Astor, and that if we have two votes against his one, he will become as powerless as an oyster. *Let us then multiply our votes;* let us call our poor but faithful Irish Catholics from every corner of the world, and gather them into the very hearts of the cities of Washington, New York, Boston, Chicago, Buffalo, Albany, Troy, Cincinnati . . . *Let no one awake those sleeping lions today. Let us pray God that they continue to sleep a few years longer, waking only to find their votes outnumbered as we will turn them forever, out of every position of honor, power and profit! . . .* What will those so-called giants think when not a single senator or member of Congress will be chosen, unless he has submitted to our holy father the pope! *We will not only elect the president, but fill and command the armies, man the navies, and hold the keys of the public treasury . . .* Then, yes! Then, we will rule the United States and lay them at the feet of the Vicar of Jesus Christ, that he may put an end to their godless system of education and impious laws of liberty of conscience, which are an insult to God and man (my italics)!"[132] The Jesuits have done everything here of which they boasted that they would do and it has mostly been done secretly behind the backs of the sleeping Americans.

And here you also see the *key* to changing the thinking of the American people and how they are able to get away with this in the United States: *EDUCATION!* The Jesuits vowed to take control of the universities and education system of American and to destroy it from the inside out. I will again quote Jesuit-trained Karl Marx, "If you control the education, *you control the people.*" Marx's goal was to bring about atheistic beliefs and to abolish the Bible in order to redefine the thinking of the people. Robert Hall said, "Wherever the Scriptures are generally read, the standard of morals is raised." We can see now how the world has become more and more evil; because the Bible ceased to be used in the school systems.

---

[132] *Fifty Years in the Church of Rome*, Charles Chiniquy, Chick Publications, pages 281, 282

In Fulton's book, *Washington in the Lap of Rome,* he divulges how the Church of Rome despised American public schools, forbid their faithful Roman Catholic followers from sending their own children to them, created parochial schools for Roman Catholic children and then flooded the public schools with Roman Catholic teachers! Here are Fulton's exact words, "The United States has established schools, where they invite the people to send their children, that they may cultivate their intelligence and become good and useful citizens. The Church of Rome has publicly cursed all these schools and forbidden their children to attend them, under pain of excommunication in this world and damnation in the next. Not only does she antagonize our school system, claiming at the outset that it bore a religious character, because the Bible found in it a welcome; but having been the cause for banishing the Word of God, she pronounces the schools godless, and sends forth the decree to have all her children housed in the parochial school, and then, with an effrontery and inconsistency that is simply astounding, she seeks to officer the schools of Protestants, so that in some of the public schools in which there is hardly a single Roman Catholic child, and where there is a parochial school in the immediate neighborhood, Rome, through suffrage obtains control of the School Board in our large cities, and then fills the schools with Roman Catholic teachers to instruct the children of Protestants. In one such school are forty-one teachers, thirty-nine of whom are Roman Catholics." Fulton also says that the Jesuits saw that "Romanism is doomed if the people of this land are to be educated . . . they understand that they are to secure the control of this continent, by destroying the public school system of America."[133]

Now, with all of the threats imposed by the Jesuits, would it be no surprise if the Jesuits are behind the "Common Core" curriculum which has enraged teachers and parents alike in 2013? This curriculum was adopted by many and most states before the School Boards even looked at a single draft of what the students would be taught. Through the $4.35 billion dollar "Race to the Top" contest, the Obama administration coerced the states into adopting "Common Core."[134]

---

[133] *Washington in the Lap of Rome,* Justin Fulton, Hard Press Publishing, 1888, pages 47-48

[134] http://www.washingtonpost.com/opinions/the-coercion-to-adopt-common-core/2013/06/14/35f088b8-d2e1-11e2-b3a2-3bf5eb37b9d0_story.html

Those states which accepted the bribe were told that when the "Common Core" curriculum was introduced in the near future, that they were to implement it into their school systems with "no questions asked." They were also partially forced into accepting the curriculum because it was only one of two ways to qualify for No Child Left Behind Act waivers. Accepting this curriculum took away the local states' rights causing the school board to be run nationally. It also lowered standards for national test scores; but because all of the national standard tests will be geared toward the "Common Core" curriculum, those who did not adopt the program will have a difficult time passing the standardized tests meaning they have *completely monopolized the entire education system!*

The "Common Core" curriculum helps to further dumb down the American students with odd senseless math techniques and assigned reading of boring material, such as, manuals which will discourage a love of reading. It also encourages them to become subservient citizens of a globalized world or New World Order. The curriculum discourages patriotism and teaches the students that Communism is good and healthy. It also introduces homosexuality and even pornography to the students.

"Common Core" also works hand in hand with Obamacare with the "Data Mining" plan being spearheaded by Bill Gates. "Data Mining" will be used to track student's grades, behavior, family values and 400 other data points used to take parent's rights away. This is an inroad for the Communistic view of "collectivism," which in this case means that children do not necessarily belong to their parents but it is the responsibility of the state to help raise the children. Remember Hillary Clinton's speech in 1996, ". . . it takes a village to raise a child?" This is not about education; it is about profit and CONTROL!

"Common Core" has been well thought out and its intentions are much more than meets the eye. According to an interview given in the early 1990's on Coast to Coast Radio, Jesuit Malachi Martin revealed that beginning in the year 1985, there was a group in Moscow called Informatik which had been drawing up what he referred to as "common curriculum" imposed by the state for high school students in Russia and in the United States with the only difference being the language. The concern then was that the values that we hold sacred here in America would be thrown out so that the common curriculum would be able to be used worldwide. Some of the values, of course, were Biblical Christianity and also patriotism to our country. The goal would be to train the young minds to accept the mindset of a New World Order. He also spoke how the education would be taken totally out of the hands of parents which would affect the "family unit" very deeply. There is no doubt in my mind that this was the beginning of the "Common Core" curriculum and that the goals are identical to the plan which began in 1985.

Justin Fulton appropriately writes, "Religious toleration has given welcome to a Jesuit priesthood that is making a religion without God and a state without liberty. They denounce the public schools, curse the Bible, murder history, and maim and mutilate literature."[135] No doubt, the Jesuits plan to devalue the Bible and destroy the United States education system has been a success. They have also been instrumental in the watering down of the Gospel in order to distract Christians from focusing on the only means for true holy living, denying oneself and looking to what Jesus accomplished on the Cross for us **(Luke 9:23-24)**! Instead we have many Church movements which focus on "self" . . . the same lie perpetrated in the Garden of Eden by Satan causing the fall of mankind **(Genesis 3:1-7)**.

The following is an excerpt from a prophecy given at the Elim Bible Institute Summer Campmeeting in 1965 by the late Stanley Frodsham. His life and ministry spanned the Pentecostal revival and he also authored the well-known book, *Smith Wigglesworth: Apostle of Faith*. He prophesied of the judgment to come which will "begin in the House of God" first. God spoke through Brother Frodsham saying:

"When I visit my people in mighty revival power, it is to prepare them for the darkness ahead. With the glory shall come great darkness, for the glory is to prepare my people for the darkness. I will enable My people to go through because of the visitation of My Spirit. Take heed to yourselves lest you be puffed up and think that you have arrived. Many shall be puffed up as in the olden days, for many then received My message but they continued not in it.

---

[135] *Washington in the Lap of Rome*, Justin Fulton, Hard Press Publishing, 1888, page 102

Did I not anoint Jehu? Yet the things I desired were not accomplished in his life. Listen to the messengers, but do not hold men's persons in admiration. For many whom I shall anoint mightily, with signs and miracles, shall be lifted up and shall fall away by the wayside. I do not do this willingly, I have made provision that they might stand. I call many into this Ministry and equip them; but remember that many shall fall. Keep your eyes upon the Lord."

"They shall be bright lights and people shall delight in them. But they shall be taken over by deceiving spirits and shall lead many of My people astray. Hearken diligently concerning these things, for in the last days will come seducing spirits that shall turn many of My anointed ones away. Many shall fall through various lusts because of sin abounding. But if you will seek Me diligently, I will put My Spirit within you. When one shall turn to the right hand or to the left you shall not turn with them, but keep your eyes wholly on the Lord."

"The coming days are most dangerous, difficult and dark, but there shall be a mighty outpouring of My Spirit upon many cities. My people must be diligently warned concerning the days that are ahead. Many shall turn after seducing spirits; many are already seducing My people. It is those who do righteousness that are righteous. Many cover their sins by theological words. But I warn you of seducing spirits who instruct My people in an evil way. Many shall come with seducing spirits and hold out lustful enticements. You will find that after I have visited My people again, the way shall become more and more narrow, and fewer shall walk therein."

"But be not deceived, the ways of righteousness are My ways. For though Satan comes as an angel of light, hearken not to him; for those who perform miracles and speak not righteousness are not of me. I warn you with great intensity that I am going to judge my house and have a Church without spot or wrinkle when I come. I desire to open your eyes and give you spiritual understanding, that you may not be deceived but may walk in uprightness of heart before Me, loving righteousness and hating every evil way."

"Look unto me, and I will make you to perceive with eyes of the Spirit the things that lurk in darkness that are not visible to the human eye. Let me lead you in this way that you may perceive the powers of darkness and

battle against them. It is not a battle against flesh and blood; for if you battle in that way, you accomplish nothing. But if you let Me take over and battle against the powers of darkness, then they are defeated and then liberation is brought to My people. I warn you to search the Scriptures diligently concerning these last days. For the things that are written shall indeed be made manifest. There shall come deceivers among My people in increasing numbers who shall speak for the truth and shall gain the favor of the people. For the people shall examine the Scriptures and say, what these men say is true. Then when they have gained the ears of the people, then and only then shall Satan enter into My people. Watch for seducers. Do you think a seducer will brandish a new heresy and flaunt it before the people? He will speak the words of righteousness and truth, and will appear as a minister of the light declaring the Word. The people's ears shall be won. Then, when the hearts are won, they will bring out their doctrines, and the people shall be deceived. The people shall say, did he not speak thus and thus? And did we not examine it from the Word? Therefore, he is a minister of righteousness. This that he has spoken we do not see in the Word, but it must be right, for the other things he spoke were true. Be not deceived. For the deceiver will first work to gain the ears of many, and then shall bring forth his insidious doctrines. You cannot discern those who are of Me and those who are not of Me when they start to preach. But seek Me constantly, and then when these doctrines are brought out you shall have a witness in your heart that these are not of Me."

"Fear not, for I have warned you. Many will be deceived. But if you walk in holiness and uprightness before the Lord, your eyes shall be opened and the Lord will protect you. If you will constantly look unto the Lord, you will know when the doctrine changes and will not be brought into it. If your heart is right I will keep you; and you will constantly look to Me, I will uphold you. The minister of righteousness shall be on this wise: his life shall agree with the Word and his lips shall give forth that which is wholly true, and it will be no mixture. When the mixture appears, then you will know he is not a minister of righteousness. The deceivers speak first the truth then error, to cover their own sins which they love. Therefore, I exhort and command you to study the Scriptures relative to seducing spirits, for this is one of the great dangers of these last days."

"I desire you firmly be established in My Word and not in the personalities of men that you will not be moved as so many shall be moved.

Take heed to yourselves and follow not the seducing spirits that are already manifesting themselves. Diligently inquire of Me when you hear something that you have not seen in My Word, and do not hold people's persons in admiration-for it is by this very method Satan will destroy many of My people."[136]

Now, I realize that this is a long prophecy and this is just an excerpt of it, but God is giving a very forthcoming warning to His people about false preachers and teachers which have most definitely come to fruition in the years since this prophecy was spoken back in 1965. What is so interesting is that the Vatican II Council was convened from 1962-1965 and this is God's warning the same year that the Council closed. I believe that is no coincidence. I have written extensively about the individuals described in this prophecy and also about the many false Church movements which have plagued the Church taking the people away from the foundation of the Bible: the Cross of Jesus Christ. God warned us in **2 Thessalonians 2:3-4** where Paul says, **"Let no man deceive you by any means: for that day shall not come, except there come a falling away first, and that man of sin be revealed, the son of perdition** (Antichrist). **Who opposes and exalts himself above all that is called God, or that he as God sits in the Temple of God, showing himself that he is God."** Those who see the deception of the enemy can see the end times fast approaching. Those who have bought into these false Church movements and whose faith has been shifted from the finished work of Jesus on the Cross to self-fulfillment may have a rude awakening when Jesus comes back for His true Church. It is not too late to repent and follow the **"strait and narrow (Matthew 7:14)"** path!

---

[136] http://www.inthebeginning.com/articles/1965prophecy.htm

Chapter Nine

SMOKESCREENS

Author and publisher, Jack Chick, gave a perfect definition of the word "smokescreens" in his 1983 manuscript bearing the same title. He so adequately wrote, "In warfare, you have enemy action. When they're moving in, they set up a smokescreen. And the smoke confuses everyone so that you don't know where your enemies are. That's one technique. The other is a fifth column where you have a country that's about to fall. So you send in agents and they wear the people down saying it's hopeless, or saying, no, the enemy isn't really going to attack. And they, in a sense, put up their own smokescreen to confuse the issue before the assault comes."[137]

The Vatican has most certainly generated various "smokescreens" to help divert attention away from their bloody past and onto other supposed threats. During the Reformation, many men such as Martin Luther, John Knox, John Calvin, as well as others; and then great Godly preachers such as Charles Finney, D. L. Moody, Charles Spurgeon and so on all believed that the Roman Catholic institution was **"the great whore"** and **"THE MOTHER OF HARLOTS"** described in the Book of Revelation.[138]

---

[137] *Smokescreens,* Jack Chick, Chick Publications, 1983, introduction
[138] *Smokescreens,* Jack Chick, Chick Publications, 1983, introduction

One reason that true Bible believing Christians today are so anemic in their faith is the fact that history has been covered up and books have been rewritten by the Jesuits. Research shows that it only takes approximately two generations for everything to be forgotten; especially if it is not told over and over again. They have attempted to do this with the many Roman Catholic inquisitions which gruesomely killed Bible believing Christians and non-Catholics. Students today do not read of these atrocities any longer. Satan has dulled our hearing and thoughts concerning crimes of the past, and most Americans cannot possibly conceive of something such as this happening here in our country.

In the book *Smokescreens*, Jack Chick documents a very informative conversation he had with the only Jesuit I have ever known to actually leave the Order after becoming born again through the blood of Jesus Christ. His name was Alberto Rivera and he was hunted down by the Jesuit Order after his departure and eventually died in 1997. God spared his life many times in order for him to expose the things he did from the time he left the Order until his death. His wife, Nury Rivera, claims with 100% accuracy that Alberto was poisoned to death. She also reveals that Vatican emissaries offered her one million dollars if she would claim that Alberto was delusional and insane while he was alive. She, of course, refused and has had many death threats herself as a result.[139] The Roman Catholic Church has tried with great hatred and fervor to discredit Alberto, but the documentation of his existence in the Jesuit Order is valid and his warnings are so pertinent for today because the information he gave is *exactly* what we are seeing happen now. Here is an excerpt of the conversation between Jack Chick and Alberto Rivera where he is speaking of information he obtained while still a member of the Jesuit Order:

Jack Chick:	What about the military picture today? How Catholic is our military position?
Alberto Rivera:	Horrifying!
Jack Chick:	What about the political picture?
Alberto Rivera:	It is even worse.
Jack Chick:	What about the Catholic structure in the judiciary?

---

[139] http://www.arcticbeacon.com/articles/7-Mar-2007.html

Alberto Rivera:	(shaking his head) It is very painful because of the heavy Jesuit penetration in this area. Most of the judicial decisions are distorting and perverting the Constitution of the United States to take away our freedoms, preparing the way for anarchy for the final take-over of the United States.
Jack Chick:	Is this preparing the way for the coming inquisition?
Alberto Rivera:	That's correct. First for anarchy. We were briefed that after all these years of penetration and infiltration, what was needed was riots and anarchy in order to finally take over. By the time the Roman Catholic Institution is ready to take over politically, militarily, educationally, and religiously, that means they will have some legal basis to do so and this will be through the concordant which has already been prepared and that is being already negotiated. I see happening right now what I was told during those briefings back in the Vatican.[140]

This interview was documented in 1983 during the presidency of Ronald Reagan who signed a concordant with the Vatican shortly after in 1984. What is a concordat? "A concordat is a pact between the Vatican and a nation-state whereby the Vatican gains certain political and financial benefits in return for support of a policy or arm of the national government. Such a concordat in a nation with numerous Catholics is also helpful in getting their allegiance or in curbing opposition to the government."[141] This concordant signed by President Reagan made the way for the Vatican to have an Embassy here in America. Now the United States has to pay a "Peter's Pence" to the Vatican which is 1/3 of what the government collects. According to some justified critics, Reagan signed "the death warrant on the United States" when this concordant was signed.

It was on January 10, 1984 when they announced that full diplomatic relations between the United States and the Vatican had been established. Signing this concordant was a direct violation of the Constitutional

---

140 *Smokescreens,* Jack Chick, Chick Publications, 1983, pages 77-78
141 Professor John M. Swomley, St. Paul School of Theology, Kansas City, Former Catholic Priest

Separation Clause. This restored relations which were suspended with extreme prejudice in 1867 after the trial of Roman Catholic John Surratt, when it was discovered positively that the Vatican and the Jesuits was directly responsible for the assassination of President Abraham Lincoln.

Did you know that Ronald Reagan's concordat and reopening of diplomatic relations with the Vatican also marked his firing of the Federal Air Traffic Controller's Union, which started a domino style labor union busting response by all the large high paying corporations and industries in this country? Shortly after the NAFTA (North American Free Trade Agreement) and GATT (General Agreement on Tariff and Trade) were signed into law and industry and corporations started to flood out of this country to set up shop in poor Roman Catholic and other Vatican controlled third world countries. This was disastrous to the economy in the United States and the employment rate of the American citizens.

Ultimately, Ronald Reagan and Pope John Paul II joined hands in the fight against the supposed common threat of Communism. Together they orchestrated the take down of the Berlin Wall. [142] I look back now and see that it was all a show and we were the audience. The sad part is that real people are involved in their devilish games.

The constant threat of Communism has been used to unite Christians and Catholics to join forces to stop it from spreading. *Communism is a smokescreen!* Russia was the seedbed of Communism under Karl Marx and Lenin who was influenced by the writings of Karl Marx. Remember that Marx was trained by the Jesuits inside the British Museum in 1848.[143] One of the goals of Communism is to breakdown the healthy family structure. Joseph Stalin, leader of the Communist Party, said, "America is like a healthy body, and its resistance is threefold, its patriotism, its morality, its spiritual life . . . If we can undermine these three areas, America will collapse from within."[144]

---

[142] http://www.freewebs.com/yahwehandtruth4/papacyoverlordoftheus.htm
[143] *Codeword Barbelon*, P. D. Stuart, Lux-Verbi Books, 2009, page 196
[144] http://www.quotesdaddy.com/quote/1401367/joseph-stalin/america-is-like-a-healthy-body-and-its-resistance

In the last chapter we briefly touched on "Common Core," the new curriculum which was deceitfully slipped into our school systems. The communistic idea of "collectivism" claims that children don't necessarily belong to their parents but it is the responsibility of the state to help raise them. It should be no surprise then that there are also involuntary mandates of "home visits" under Obamacare where social workers will determine if you are raising your child or children according to the new states standards, and if you are not, they will take your children away into the custody of the state. Bible believing Christians will be seen as dangerous because teaching the Bible is "indoctrinating" our children to be "close-minded" and "intolerant" of the issues in the world which are obviously forbidden in the Word of God and condemned as sin. One article states, "Intervention may be with any family for any reason. It may also result in the child or children being required to go to certain schools or taking certain medications and vaccines and even having more limited- or no-interaction with parents. The federal government will now set the standards for raising children and will enforce them by home visits." Over $224 million dollars has been allocated toward these home visits.[145]

We must remember that a true faithful Roman Catholic believes in their heart that their Church is the *only* true Church of Jesus Christ. They believe that the pope is the vicar, or representative, of Jesus Christ on this Earth. The teaching of "Temporal Power" means that the pope should control *every person on the face of this Earth*; their property and their choice of religion. The Jesuits, as the strong-arm of Rome, are pushing for this Temporal Power which means a worldwide dictator will take control. Let us look again at Pope Benedict XVI, who issued the "*Caritas in Veritate* (Charity in Truth)" encyclical before leaving office claiming that a "World Political Authority" was necessary in order to "manage the global economy; to revive economies hit by the crisis; to avoid any deterioration of the present crisis and the greater imbalances that would result; to bring about integral and timely disarmament, food security and peace; to guarantee the protection of the environment and to regulate migration . . ."

---

[145] http://www.examiner.com/article/report-obamacare-provision-will-allow-forced-home-inspections-by-gov-t-agents

Pope Benedict XVI calls for "timely disarmament," which would leave Americans unable to defend themselves against a tyrant government. I truly believe that with the facts which have come forward outside of the mainstream media, the most current mass shootings were intentionally perpetrated to cause alarm among Americans and vilify guns so that the American people would be convinced to turn in their weapons. It worked in many large cities because people were lined up for miles dumping their guns in waste bins. In the Los Angeles Times, a story reported that people were turning in their guns in exchange for gift cards![146]

What many and most people do not realize is that the Roman Catholic Church has not changed her power hungry mentality. The Vatican absolutely abhors the United States of America! She condemned the Declaration of Independence as "wickedness" and called the Constitution of the United States a "satanic document!"[147] Why? Because the Constitution affords every human being with freedom and liberty of conscience, which is declared by all the popes and councils of Rome as, "a most godless, unholy, and diabolical thing, which every good Catholic must abhor and destroy at any cost."[148]

Here is some relevant history of the Vatican's past which has been swept under the rug. The bloody St. Bartholomew massacre took place on August 24, 1572 with the purpose being to destroy the Protestant movement in France after the Reformation had begun. The king of France had cleverly arranged a marriage between his sister and Henry of Navarre, head of the Protestant army. There was a great feast with much celebrating and after four days of feasting, the soldiers were given a signal and at an hour before dawn, all the houses of the Protestant's in the city were forced open at once. Admiral Coligny, the chief Protestant leader, was killed and his body was thrown out of a window into the street where his head was cut off and sent to the pope. They also cut off his arms and private parts and dragged him through the streets for three days until

---

[146] http://articles.latimes.com/2006/nov/26/local/me-compton26
[147] Avro Manhattan, "The Dollar and the Vatican", Ozark Book Publishers, 1988, page 26.
[148] *Fifty Years in the Church of Rome,* Charles Chiniquy, Chick Publications, 1985, page 284

they finally hung his dead body by the heels outside of the city. They also slaughtered many other well-known Protestants and within the first three days over 10,000 people were killed. Some bodies were thrown into the river and as blood ran through the streets into the river, it appeared like a stream of blood. They even slew their own followers if they suspected that they were not very strong in their beliefs or if they were sympathetic to the Protestants. From Paris, the destruction spread to all parts of the country and over 8000 more people were killed. [149]

A similar massacre occurred in Ireland in the year 1641. The conspirators planned a general uprising for the whole country on October 23rd, the feast of Ignatius Loyola, the founder of the Jesuit Order. The plan was that all Protestants would be killed at once. To throw them off guard while the plan was being made, extra acts of kindness were shown to the Protestants. Early in the morning of October 23rd, the conspirators were armed and every Protestant they could catch was immediately murdered. They showed absolutely no mercy as small children to the defenseless elderly were killed. Even invalids were not spared! The Protestants were caught by complete surprise because they had lived in peace and safety for years. They were massacred by neighbors, friends, and even relatives. Death often was the least they had to fear because the methods of torture were downright sadistic. Women were tied to posts and their tops were stripped down to the waist while their breasts were cut off with large shears and they were left to bleed to death. Pregnant women were tied to tree branches as their unborn babies were cut out and fed to hungry dogs; all while their husbands were forced to watch! What you have just read here is documented and historically factual material found in *Foxes Book of Martyrs*. Please look how these murderous assaults by the Vatican against the Christians in France and in Ireland followed a similar pattern. Before the attacks, there was a time of peace when the Roman Catholics became friendly and warm, and in both cases the Christians were so relieved that they let their guard down and assumed the Vatican had changed. This was their fatal mistake and it cost them their lives! [150]

---

[149] Smokescreens, Jack Chick, Chick Publications, 1983, page 14

[150] *Smokescreens*, Jack Chick, Chick Publications, 1983, page 17

How would one classify Adolf Hitler? It seems to me that most decent human beings would see Hitler as an absolute monster. I couldn't agree more, but do you remember that Hitler was a faithful Roman Catholic until the day he died. Here again is an excerpt from his eulogy given on the day of his supposed death, May 3, 1945: "Adolf Hitler, son of the Catholic Church, died while defending Christianity (Catholicism) . . . words cannot be found to lament over his death . . . Over his mortal remains stands his victorious moral figure. With the palm of the martyr God gives Hitler the laurels of victory."[151] Hitler had said, "As for the Jews, I am just carrying on with the same policy which the Catholic Church has adopted for 1500 years, when it has regarded the Jews as dangerous and push them into ghettos etc., because it knew what the Jews were like. I don't put race about religion, but I do see the danger in the representatives of this race for Church and State, and perhaps I am doing Christianity a great service."[152] World War II was basically a Roman crusade against Jews, Orthodox and Protestants under the cover of politics! To recap, after World War II, most of the world knew that the Vatican was responsible for the atrocities which took place. So in 1962 the Vatican II Council was created and the **"MOTHER OF HARLOTS"** had a facelift. She claimed that the Protestant "heretics" were now to be called "separated brethren," and she also claimed that Catholics should now be called "Christians." How utterly deceptive; unfortunately it had a massive impact on true Christianity today!

Let us look at how a harlot seduce her victims? **Proverbs 7:6-10, 22,24,27** says, **"I discerned among the youths, a young man boy that understanding, passing through the street near her corner; and he went the way to her house, in the twilight, in the evening, in the black and dark night: And behold, there met him a woman with the attire of a harlot, and subtle of heart . . . With her much fair speech she caused him to yield, with the flattering of her lips she forced him. He goes after her straightway, as an ox goes to the slaughter. Hearken unto me now therefore, oh you children, and attend to the words of my mouth. Let not your heart declined to go**

---

[151] *Secret History of the Jesuits*, Edmond Paris, Chick Publications—translated from French in 1975, page 162

[152] *Smokescreens*, Jack Chick, Chick Publications, 1983, page 23

her ways, go not astray in her paths. For she has cast down many wounded: yes, many strongmen have been slain by her. Her house is the way to Hell, going down to the chambers of death." The Bible says the "**MOTHER OF HARLOTS**" will seduce kings and nations with her cunning and that the nations have been made drunk, which means they are confused, disoriented, unstable, and can be easily deceived and conquered by her **(Revelation 17:1-6)**.

Following World War II, the Vatican launched an anti-communist attack using Bishop Fulton J. Sheen. This shift focused on Communism and took the eyes off the Vatican; an excellent use of the smokescreen tactic, especially considering that the Roman Catholic Church had created this "run-away child" called Communism in the first place. Many disguised Jesuits were planted in the Protestant denominations and Protestants seminaries to change the focus of the message going forth. The Gospel began to become watered-down and a push for "unity" was encouraged. Anti-Catholic sermons were discouraged and frowned upon across the nation. What began to take place was a subtle but extremely dangerous shift from exposing the **"harlot"** of the Book of Revelation to a unity of faith and an ecumenical spirit which has truly changed Christianity. We are hard-pressed to find a Church which preaches the true Gospel anymore in our cities. There are plenty of Churches, and some are very large "mega" Churches, but most people in the congregations are hearing a watered-down social Gospel of self-help and Humanistic Psychology. It is all about "self" and not about "denying self" as Jesus instructed in **Luke 9:23-24**. The religion of humanism says that *man is divine* which could not be further from the truth! Man is separated from God because of sin and the only way to deal with the sin problem is through accepting the death of Jesus Christ on the Cross which frees us from the penalty and the power of sin.

This subtle shift in the Gospel message did not happen randomly, it has been slowly perpetuated by the Jesuits and the Church of Rome. Please understand why this is so damaging and why true Bible believing Christians are so disheartened by this move. The Bible clearly teaches us in several of its Books that a man, which the Bible calls "**Antichrist**" or "**the Beast**" will come and deceive the majority of the world. Antichrist will be the leader of a one world government and in order for this government to succeed, it will need a one world religion. The Bible describes the leader of this one world religion as the **"false prophet"** and he will have a great power to perform signs and miracles which will deceive the masses of people **(Revelation 13:11-18).** He will cause the misled people to worship **"the Beast"** and to take "the mark of the Beast." Those who will not accept this mark will not be able to buy or sell.

One very important scheme of the Jesuits is to target those who are preaching the pure Word of God and to cause them to stumble and fall before the world. I have seen this in my own lifetime on many occasions. The Jesuits, in disguise as "brothers in Christ," surround these Godly ministers and their ministries and make sure to cause havoc. The goal being to either change the message going forth, using smokescreens often times and/or by discrediting the minister using scandalous methods. Remember this portion of the Jesuit oath which reads, "My son, heretofore you have been taught to act the *dissembler* . . . among Protestants, generally to be a Protestant, and obtaining their confidence, to seek even to preach from their pulpits . . . that you might be enabled to gather together all information for the benefit of your Order as a faithful soldier of the pope (my italics)."

As P.D. Stuart, author of *Codeword Barbelon*, so aptly stated, "THE JESUIT ALWAYS ACCOMPLISHES HIS PURPOSE, for this creature can metamorphose himself into any form to accomplish his purpose. He can develop his powers of adaptation to suit the preferences of those whom he wishes to influence or whose confidence he desires to possess, the Jesuits with the Pagans be a pagan, with the atheist he will be an atheist, or a liberal, with the Jews he will be a Jew, and with the reformers he will be a reformer—even an Evangelical. In whatever place or vocation he be found, the Jesuit is always a *double man*, with two distinct missions—one public and the other secret."[153]

Another alarming tidbit of information is that the Department of Homeland Security has been stockpiling ammunition at increasing rates! It was confirmed that besides the already 1.6 *billion* rounds of

---

[153] *Codeword Barbelon*, P.D. Stuart, Lux-Verbi Books, 2009, page 215

ammunition purchased in just ten months, the DHS also purchased another 21.6 million rounds. To put it in proper perspective, the war on Iraq used around 70 million rounds per year. That is a lot of ammunition being bought, not to mention the massive amounts of firearms they are purchasing.[154] What is even more frightening is that some of this ammunition is specifically designed for high powered *foreign* weapons. The interesting thing is that we have willingly allowed United Nations[155] and Russian troops on American soil as a part of FEMA training supposedly for joint anti-terrorism drills.[156] The troops are being trained in search and seizure, as well as, controlling of mass populations.[157] Under Posse Comitatus Act, the federal statute makes it illegal to employ any members of the United States army for the purpose of executing laws, unless such a use of force was authorized expressly by the Constitution or Congress. I suppose the use of foreign troops to enforce martial law is their loop hole around the dilemma.

The following is an expose' written concerning the Department of Homeland Security printed in the Canada Free Press. It is an eye opener showing how all of this is coming full circle as the planning phase is being completed! This DHS insider is retiring along with many others inside DHS who don't like what the agency has become. In his words, he states, "DHS and other organizations have become the private army of the Oval Office . . . DHS is like a prison environment, complete with prison snitches . . . and the warden is obsessed. Ask anyone in DHS. No one trusts anyone else and whatever sources might be left are shutting up. The threats that have been made far exceed anything I've ever seen. Good people are afraid for their lives and the lives of their families. We've all been threatened. They see the writing on the wall and are leaving. It's not a joke and not hype."

The following is a narrative from the journalist's source explaining the plan for the takeover of the United States: "According to every

[154] http://www.forbes.com/sites/ralphbenko/2013/03/11/1-6-billion-rounds-of-ammo-for-homeland-security-its-time-for-a-national-conversation/
[155] http://www.thedailysheeple.com/where-is-the-proof-that-un-soldiers-are-on-american-soil-oh-right-here_082012
[156] http://www.inquisitr.com/828674/russian-troops-on-american-soil-confirmed/
[157] http://www.thedailysheeple.com/where-is-the-proof-that-un-soldiers-are-on-american-soil-oh-right-here_082012

internal document I've seen and read, and from the few people I've spoken with who understand what's going on, preparations have been finalized to respond to a crisis of unprecedented magnitude within the United States. The response will include the use of lethal force against U.S. citizens under the instructions of Barack Obama." When asked by the journalist, "But why?" he responded, "The crisis will be rooted in an economic collapse. I told you last year, at a time when gold and silver were setting record highs, one specific indicator that time is very short. It is the final 'smack down' of the metals, gold and silver, that will presage the orchestrated economic collapse that is being planned by the bankers of Wall Street. Everybody needs to understand that this is a deliberate collapse of the U.S. economy with the oversight of the White House and the full knowledge of the Justice Department. Everyone seems to be waiting for some big, history making event that will signal the start of the collapse. The fact is that the collapse has already started. It's incremental, like a snowball rolling down a hill. It gets bigger and rolls faster. Well, this snowball is well on its way down the hill."

He goes on to say, "I don't mean to sound repetitive, but I can't stress this enough. Contrary to what you hear, we're already in an economic collapse, except that most people haven't a clue. The 'big bang' comes at the end, when people wake up one morning and can't log in to their bank accounts, can't use their ATM cards, and find out that their private pension funds and other assets have been confiscated. I've seen documentation of multiple scenarios created outside of DHS. Different plans and back-up plans. Also, please understand that I deliberately used the word 'created,' as this is a completely manufactured event. In the end it won't be presented that way, which is extremely important for everyone to understand. What is coming will be blamed on some unforeseen event out of everyone's control that few saw coming or thought would actually happen. Then, another event will take place concurrent with this event, or immediately after it, to confuse and compound an already explosive situation."

The insider explains, "As I said, there are several scenarios and I don't know them all. I know one call for a cyber-attack by an external threat, which will then be compounded by something far removed from everyone's own radar. But it's all a ruse, or a pretext. The threat is from within. Before people can regain their footing, a second event will be triggered . . . . I've seen one operational plan that refers to the federal government's response to a significant terrorist attack on U.S. soil. Information at these levels is compartmentalized. I don't have specifics, just plans for the response. The response will be controls and restrictions on travel, business, and every aspect of our lives, especially gun ownership and speech that incites people against the government. I guess some people would call it martial law, and they would not be incorrect. But understand that this will be a process deployed in stages. How quickly of a process remains to be seen . . . Please note a few final things. The relationship that exists between DHS today and the executive branch is well beyond alarming. DHS and other organizations have become the private army of the Oval Office. The NSA, and I've got contacts there, is taking orders from the Oval Office. The IRS is under the virtual control of the Oval Office in a manner that would make Nixon cower. Even though all roads appear to lead to the Oval Office, they lead through the Oval Office. It's not just Obama, but the men behind him, the people who put him there. The people who put him there are the ones who created him."

The journalist then asks "who created Obama." The insider answers, "First, ask yourself why there was such an all-out effort to marginalize anyone talking about Obama's eligibility in 2008. Even so-called conservatives pundits fell for the lie that such questions were nothing more than a diversion. They were following a specific drumbeat. That should tell every rational adult that he is a creation of the globalists who have no allegiance to any political party. He is the product of decades of planning, made for this very time in our history. He was selected to oversee the events I just disclosed . . . As often said by another of my sources, the U.S. is a captured operation. The lie is bigger than most people realize or are willing to confront. That is, until there is no other option. By then, it might be too late."[158]

This article confirms the need for FEMA camps and even points to specific events which are planned by who he refers to as "globalists," but we can take it a step further and conclude that these globalists are Jesuits.

[158] Canada Free Press http://thelastgreatstand.com/lgs/2013/12/29/dhs-insider-everyone-seems-to-be-waiting-for-some-big-history-making-event/

The object being the implementation of a New World Order, which has been in the making for a very long time. They have never been closer to fulfilling this goal than now. After World War I, President Woodrow Wilson pushed the United States to join the League of Nations which the people of this great nation did not consent. President Wilson was under the control of a Jesuit named Colonel Edward Mandell House. Woodrow Wilson said about his relationship with Colonel House, "Mr. House is my second personality. He is my independent self. His thoughts and mine are one."[159] Wilson was completely overshadowed by Colonel House and it was written, "For seven long years, Colonel House was Woodrow Wilson's other self. For six long years he shared with him everything but the title of Chief Magistracy of the Republic. For six years, two rooms were at his disposal in the north wing of the White House. It was House who made the slate for the Cabinet, formulated the first policies of the Administration, and practically directed the foreign affairs of the United States."[160]

When World War I did not produce the desired results for the Jesuits of a unified world government under papal rule because the United States failed to join the League of Nations, then another war was necessary which would have the people crying out for peace and a united nations. Actually, the League of Nations was a forerunner to the United Nations which was set up after World War II. Also, the Vatican and the Jesuits still wanted to retaliate for their defeat in World War I. As Abraham Lincoln said, "The Jesuits never forgive nor forsake [give up]."[161] World War II was the most devastating war in history in regards to lives lost, to destruction and to economic ruin!

Paul Warburg, architect for the Federal Reserve and member of Council on Foreign Relations, said on February 17, 1950 in an address to the U.S. Senate, "We shall have a world government, whether or not we like it. The only question is whether world government will be achieved by *conquest or consent* (my italics)." At this point it may very well be

---

[159] *The Intimate Papers of Colonel House*, Charles Seymour, Houghton Mifflin, Vol. I, pages. 114-115

[160] Viereck, The Strangest Friendship in History - Woodrow Wilson and Colonel House 1932

[161] *Fifty Years in the Church of Rome*, Charles Chiniquy, Chick Publications, 1985, page 281

achieved by *the consent* of blinded individuals if the citizens of the United States do not wake up!

In 1991, George H.W. Bush said in his state of the union address, "It is a big idea: a New World Order, where diverse nations are drawn together in a common cause to achieve the universal aspirations of mankind: peace and security, freedom and the rule of law."[162] Several years later in January of 2004, CNN reported that, "Pope John Paul II rang in the New Year on Thursday with a renewed call for peace in the Middle East and Africa and the creation of a New World Order . . ."[163] In Pope Benedict XVI's 2005 Christmas message, he called for a "New World Order" and a "united humanity."[164]

Please do not be fooled by the false peace which is promised by a New World Order! This is a grand deception which has caused many to jump on board this sinking ship. The true existence of a New World Order would be under a fascist dictator, Antichrist, who would rule the world and a great mass of suppressed and controlled people of all nations and tongues. *This is not about world peace; this is about absolute and complete CONTROL over all of mankind.*

Another smokescreen that really has Americans talking is the threat of the religion of Islam here in America. The people of the Islamic religion, called Muslims, refer to the United States of America as "the Great Satan" and Israel as "the Lesser Satan." The Islamic religion believes in spreading the words of their sacred book, the Quran, by the sword. This means that they *will* and *do* kill those who refuse to convert to Islam. Like the Roman Catholic Church, they too want to convert the entire world to their religion and they are not opposed to fighting a holy war, called "jihad," to accomplish their goal of world dominance.

Islam is extremely exclusive and the people of Islam are very loyal to their religion. There is no evangelization within any of the predominantly Muslim countries. The Saudi government states that all citizens *must be* Muslim and will only allow religious minorities to enter the country as

---

[162] President George Bush, State of the Union address, January 29. 1991

[163] http://www.cuttingedge.org/News/n2020.cfm

[164] Benedict XVI, "Christmas Message," ZENIT, December 25, 2005

temporary workers. These minorities are not allowed to openly practice their faith in public places or proselytize in any way. [165]

The Muslims have a jihad tactic where they move into a land as a minority and then begin to multiply their followers at a swift pace. While many families these days may have an average of two or three children, Muslims are allowed to marry up to *four wives* at a time and therefore the number of children they may produce is exceedingly more than the average American family. The actual average number of children per family is 8.1 for Muslims and about 1.6-2.1 for Americans.[166] Osama bin Laden was one of fifty-three children and he sired twenty-seven children.[167] Even if Osama bin Laden's fifty-two brothers and sisters produced only *half* of the number of children in which he did, this would still equal approximately 730 grandchildren for his own parents! My point is that even just a few hundred Muslims in one community can grow so quickly that it could change the demographics of that community. A dramatic population change such as this could result in a terrifying power shift, which has happened to many other countries which the Muslims have taken over by force.

Islam is not only a religion, but it is also a culture or a way of life for Muslims. It mimics the culture of 7th century Arabia when a so-called prophet, Muhammad, was said to be receiving visions from Allah, which Muslims believe to be God. Allah is actually the personal name which the pagans used for the moon god. This is the same god whom they prayed to while facing Mecca, as the Muslims do to this very day, because the statue of Allah was actually located there.[168] Muhammad created the religion of Islam and has used much force and violence to convert others. This is the same way in which the Muslims operate to this very day. The followers believe that this is the way in which they will get to "Paradise," which is the Islamic word for Heaven. "Paradise" is described as having all of the "lusts of the flesh" which are forbidden here on this Earth. They are taught from birth to spread the words of the Quran by the sword, and to kill any "infidels (un-believers)" who deny that Allah is God. A person

---

[165] http://en.wikipedia.org/wiki/Saudi_Arabia#Demographics
[166] http://www.awakengeneration.com/thoughts/beheard/998
[167] *Because They Hate*, Brigitte Gabriel, St. Martin's Press, New York, 2006, page16
[168] http://www.biblebelievers.org.au/islam.htm

has only two choices: you can either *convert to Islam* or *die*. Does this sound identical to *another religion's* way of forced conversions.

After Muhammad's death, his followers took many of his visions and put them on paper, thereby creating the Quran, the sacred book of Islam. The Muslims are taught from a very young age to hate anyone who a non-Muslim and they also have a particular distaste for Jews and true Christians. Surah 5:51 of the Quran says, "Believers, take not Jews and Christians for your friends . . ." If a Muslim kills a non-Muslim in the name of Allah, then it is believed that the victim's death is a gift for Allah. Many people believe that Muslims are worshiping the same God in which the Christians and Jews worship. This is simply not true so please do not be fooled. Just because they worship one god does not mean that it is the same God that we worship.

Now that we have established some basic facts about Islam and the practices and beliefs of their followers known as Muslims, let's ask the question, "Could Islam be a tool of Rome?" Let us look a little deeper into the formation of the religion in the 7th century and see if we can discover any similarities between Islam and Roman Catholicism.

Muhammad was born in 570 A.D. and died in 632 A.D. The Quran was written in 650 A. D. This time in history was a time when true Christianity had been spreading in the Middle East as a result of the preaching of the Gospel of Jesus Christ. Remember also that by this time period, the Roman Catholic religion had become very organized and the pope of Rome, probably still referred to as "the Bishop of Rome," would have been working diligently to convert the entire world to the state religion of Roman Catholicism with the desire to be the head and sole ruler of the entire temporal world.

Some will be quite surprised to learn that Muhammad was a Roman Catholic before he created this diabolical religion of Islam and his distorted views of God's Word are found within the pages of the Quran and the Hadith. He married Kjadija when he was just 25 years old and she was 40 years old. Kjadija came from a very wealthy family and also came out of a Roman Catholic convent. Many claim that she was even a nun![169]

Basically, through Muhammad, the Roman Catholic Church created Islam to destroy true Christians and Jews and to capture the prized Holy Land of Jerusalem for the pope. For the first few hundred years of their existence, Islam did just that. When it came time for the powerful generals of the Islamic armies to surrender Jerusalem to the pope, they refused to give it up because they realized the great power which they had attained. Thus, the papacy created the Crusades, carried out by the fierce Knights Templar Order, to drive the Islamic forces out of Jerusalem and to establish the throne of the pope in Jerusalem. Rome waged nine Crusades for two centuries, beginning in 1095 AD and ending in 1302 AD but the Knights were not able to push the Muslims out. Islam maintained control of Jerusalem for over six centuries until they were captured by the British in World War I and the land was handed over to King George V, a prominent Knights of Malta.

The plans of the pope did not play out in his favor this particular time in history, but what control does the papacy of the Roman Catholic Church have over the religion of Islam today? While, many people recognize the threat of Islam in America and in the world, others are completely oblivious to it. Many claim that the President of the United States, Barack Hussein Obama, is a Muslim in disguise attempting to set up Sharia Law here in America. I believe to make such a statement, the facts need to be laid out and assessed.

While this book has primarily been about the desire of the pope of the Roman Catholic Church to be sole ruler of the temporal world and the Jesuits role in helping him achieve this goal, I have taken page after page to show that the Jesuits are in control of our government, education, press and media here in the United States. I have also attempted to prove their power within the world to control every committee, organization, parliament, secret society, council, etc. It is not the Muslims who head up and control the European Union, the United Nations, the Council on Foreign Relations, the Bilderbergs, the Freemasons, the armed forces

---

[169] Walter J. Veith- *The Islamic -Catholic Connection- Total Onslaught series*

around the world, the universities and colleges all over the world, etc. And if you will remember, Islamic leaders such as Yasser Arafat and Saddam Hussein were trained by the Jesuits in Jesuit schools! These are examples of some of the leaders of the Islamic religion who ultimately pay their respects and bow down to the Jesuit General!

The Jesuits will use "threats" so that the people will accept any changes which are necessary to meet the threat. Is it possible that the religion of Islam and terrorism is yet another way to scare the people of the United States into accepting "change" just to protect themselves? After the 9/11 attacks on the World Trade Center and the Pentagon, the first response of the Jesuit-controlled media was that we are under a threat from the enemy and that we may have to *surrender some of our freedoms* which we hold dear to us as Americans to keep us safe. *The main purpose of the World Trade Center tragedy was to scare the American citizens into giving up their freedoms and to implement measures to legally spy on citizens.*

Many do not want to accept the fact that there is overwhelming evidence that the World Trade Center collapse was an inside job. From the explosive nano-thermite composite material used to implode buildings found in the dust by an international team of scientists, to the fact that over 100 first-responders reported explosions and flashes at the onset of destruction. Right now, over one thousand architects and engineers are calling for a new 9/11 investigation because of the overwhelming evidence pointing to fact that the skyscrapers were demolished with explosives.[170]

This is what the newspapers were saying after the 9/11 attacks: "Tighter Security Means Less Freedom," was the title of this article written the day after the attacks which stated, "Experts, however, say there is much work to be done. And it will involve much more spending and planning, hardening of key facilities and, perhaps, higher taxes and forfeiture of some *personal freedoms.*"[171] Another article stated, "As the United States faces a new war against uncertain and hidden enemies, the temptation to *sacrifice our freedom* in the hopes of protecting ourselves from harm is powerful." What about this article entitled, "Freedom or Safety?" which stated, "Anti-terrorism measures may mean *forfeiture*

---

[170] http://news.yahoo./s/usnw/20100219/pl_usnw/DC57612_1
[171] Orlando Sentinel, Wednesday, September 12th

of some personal freedoms."[172] And lastly, "The *constitutional protections of speech and privacy* that Americans value so highly reflect a balance between individual liberty and state security. Just how those lines are drawn, history teaches, is directly affected by the perceived threats to our country's security."

The 9/11 attacks, as well as the most recent terrorists attacks are a test of the American people. Would the citizens of the United States be willing to sacrifice their freedoms to protect themselves from the threat of terrorism? Who gets the blame for these terrorists' activities? The *radical Muslims* do. But as we have already stated, the Islamic terrorists groups such as Al Qaeda, Hamas and Hezbollah are all financed by the money earned through the international drug trafficking which is orchestrated by the Jesuit General through the CIA and the Mafia. Both the CIA and the Mafia are run by the Knights of Malta, a Roman Catholic Order and by the very prominent and wealthy Roman Catholic nobility families referred to as the "Black Nobility." If the people of the world will look through the "smokescreen," they will see the Jesuit General pulling the strings!

Now that we have established that Muhammad was a Roman Catholic before he began his Islamic religion and the purpose of creating such a religion, we can look at the similarities between Islam and Roman Catholicism:

- Catholicism and Islam stand side by side in all of the Islamic countries. Where there is a mosque, many times there will be a Roman Catholic cathedral nearby. Both will often have *a sun* depicted on the gates of their churches.
- If you will remember, there is no evangelization within the predominately Islamic countries; however, you will not hear any complaining by the hierarchy of the Roman Catholic Church. Why? It is because their purposes are one and the same and they are working together behind the scenes to make it happen.
- Both Islam and Catholicism encourage pilgrimages for the faithful. *This is a pagan practice!*

---

[172] Orlando Sentinel, Wednesday, September 12th

- The Jesuits believe like the Muslims that they will be glorified in the courts of Heaven, according to the quality of his deeds of martyrdom.
- Neither of the two religions have any problem with building their cathedrals or mosques on old pagan sites. Some of these sights have the male phallic symbol displayed everywhere, yet there is an Islamic mosque attached to the old site or a Roman Catholic Cathedral right next to it.
- In the Freemason's book, *Morals and Dogmas*, it states that the crescent (the moon) and disk (the sun) combined always represent the conjunctive sun and moon, meaning the sun and moon in the act of reproduction. This is representative of the male and female deity which ties these symbols to the fertility cults. This is also known as Baal worship and deep down as Luciferian worship or worship of Satan. It can also be depicted as the crescent moon representing the uterus of the female giving birth to the sun god. This symbol is seen all of Islamic flags, mosques and statues, as well as, it is seen all over the Roman Catholic Churches and even used in their monstrance's which actually houses the wafer god they call "Jesus." You will see the sunburst monstrance and inside will be a crescent moon lying on its side to hold the sun god wafer.
- Roman Catholicism uses the same 8-sided star that Islam does. It is representative of two squares overlapping or the male and female deity again in the conjunctive state.
- Woman in Islam are seen as inferior to men. They have their own areas in the mosque where they must congregate and do not mingle with the men. Women in Roman Catholicism are not allowed to become priests. Muslim woman also dress almost identical to Roman Catholic nuns.
- Both Islam and Roman Catholicism use prayer beads.
- In Islam, the "all-seeing eye" is very prominent. It is also used in the architecture of many Roman Catholic Churches, sometimes in a pyramid with the sun burst behind it just like on the back of the American dollar bill. This eye is the eye of Osiris or Satan!

St. Peter's Basilica-
Vatican

Catholic Cathedral
in Milano, Italy

Back of the one
dollar bill

- The Quran teaches that we came into existence through evolution. The last two popes, along with others, believe that "Christianity and evolution are compatible."[173] Pope John Paul II said on October 23, 1996 that evolution is "more than just a theory."[174]
- Both Ignatius Loyola, the founder of the Jesuit Order, and Muhammad received their "revelations" in a cave. Ironically, you will almost always see Mary statues in a cave in front of Roman Catholic Churches and also in the statues found in the yards of faithful Roman Catholics.
- Both Islam and Roman Catholicism believe in the immaculate conception of Mary (that she was born without sin), her purity (that she is a perpetual virgin) and according to Roman Catholic Bishop Fulton Sheen, "the two largest religions in the world believe in fervent devotion to Mary and hold her virtues in the very highest esteem."[175]

Ultimately, the Jesuit General still has the upper hand in the religion of Islam. As stated before, we know that Saddam Hussein and other high ranking Islamic leaders are Jesuit trained and are also 33rd degree Freemasons, which means that their agenda is the same: a New World Order! It is the demonic plan of Satan. Remember that both Roman Catholicism and Islam want world dominance, but they do not seem to be fighting one another for it. One must ask the why? It is because of the

[173] http://www.allheadlinenews.com/articles/7014059195
[174] http://www.bible.ca/tracks/b--accepts-evolution.htm
[175] http://www.heartsare.com

fact that the Jesuit General knows that he has the Islamic leaders in his pocket.

Let's look at another important smokescreen being used to attempt to unite the world on a common global threat. Does the term "Global Warming" ring a bell? Global warming refers to an unequivocal and continuing rise in the average temperature of Earth's climate system. It was promoted by Al Gore's documentary titled, "An Inconvenient Truth" which warned the world of the severity of the so-called climate crisis and even earned him a Nobel Peace Prize. This global warming scare has been proven a hoax by many in the science world, yet the instigators of the trend refuse to debate the scientists on the facts which completely deflate the Global Warming theory. This theory goes hand in hand with the U.N. sustainability push, "carbon footprint" warnings, and the "Green" movement which has flooded our lives. Most of us care deeply about the planet and do not want to see it destroyed, but these movements have little to do with pollution and energy conservation and more to do with *control*. The Roman Catholic Church, of course, is deeply involved. Cardinal Theodore McCarrick was quoted as saying that Catholic bishops will be promoting a new "Climate Covenant" and "take the message on the seriousness of climate change to every Catholic parish in America." A related organization is the Catholic Climate Covenant, which claims that the poor are suffering because of the "carbon footprints" of people in the United States and other "rich" nations. *America Magazine*, the national Catholic weekly published by the Jesuits, said, "If the planet is to survive, as Pope Benedict XVI concluded in Caritas in Veritate, all nations must accept binding reductions in carbon emissions and construct an equitable structure for energy consumption and for sharing the development of green technology among rich and poor nations—for the sake of this generation and generations to come."[176] Looks like more measures to control our lives. They will use devices such as these "smart meters" being installed in our homes to measure natural gas and water consumption. Once you have used up your allotted amount of resources for the month, your house will basically shut down until the following month!

---

[176] http://newswithviews.com/Kincaid/cliff375.htm

No doubt, there are countless other smokescreens being used to divert the attention of the people so that the Jesuits can move forward with the plan of world dominance without many even suspecting it! Jack Chick pleads with the pastors and the people of America at the end of his 1983 book, *Smokescreens,* to remember the past and to keep history from being repeated again. He so poignantly says, ". . . If you don't turn into a soul winning Church, the whore is going to have you and your grandchildren for breakfast. Have you already forgotten the screams that filled the night air in Paris during the St. Bartholomew massacre? Have you forgotten the little pregnant mothers tied to the tree branches, begging for mercy in Ireland while the dogs were fighting underneath for their unborn children? And the bloody knives in the hands of those smirking fanatics driven on by their priests to butcher these Christian ladies? Have you forgotten these bloodbaths that were quoted in *Foxes Book of Martyrs?* The Vatican wants you to forget it. Have you forgotten what took place in Yugoslavia . . . Catholic priests impaling children on stakes as they screamed in agony in 1940? You better *never* forget it! And don't forget that it was at a time of peace, love and kindness just before each attack, just like today, beloved. And don't you forget the one million Knights of Columbus in the United States have sworn to turn America into a papal state. God help us. You don't think it's coming here? You don't think history repeats itself? It's time to get sober and turn into spiritual soldiers, and start arming yourselves with the helmet of salvation and the shield of faith, and the sword of the Spirit, realizing the forces of darkness can be held back."[177]

---

[177] *Smokescreens,* Jack Chick, Chick Publications, 1983, page 90

A WOLF IN SHEEP'S CLOTHING

When Pope Benedict XVI stepped down on February 28, 2013, which occurred only *once* in the history of the Roman Catholic Church, those of us who enjoy eschatology were practically holding our breath in anticipation of what would happen next. Even I was stunned to see these headlines posted on March 13, 2013: ***Francis I, First Jesuit Pope in Vatican History***! Jorge Mario Bergoglio, *a Jesuit*, was elected as the pope of Rome! Now, knowing what we do of the Jesuit Order and its desire to control the world using the White Pope as its public figurehead, it was quite astounding to see a Jesuit take the papal throne. And not only did the first Jesuit ever in history secure this position, but this man who they call "Pope Francis" has become the world's newest super hero! He has been seen on the cover of *Time Magazine* as "Person of the Year" and even recently appeared on the cover of *Rolling Stone Magazine*! I personally hear and see people of all faiths and religious backgrounds heralding praises to him for his "meek" and "humble" demeanor. I will say that quite possibly Pope Francis could be the key to binding all false religions and bring the "unity" the world so seeks.

Let us look at the popularity of this pope since his election in March of 2013. The headlines in the mainstream media and in print recorded:

Francis drew 6.6 million to Vatican in 2013, three times Benedict. [178]
The article stated, "More than 6.6 million people attended events with
Pope Francis at the Vatican from his election in March to the end of
2013, figures released on Thursday showed, compared to 2.3 million for
former Pope Benedict in all of 2012. The Vatican said the figures were
based on the number of tickets issued for papal events where they are
needed, such as general audiences, Masses and private audiences. They
were also based on estimates of the number of people at events where
tickets are not needed, such as his weekly appearance from a window
overlooking St. Peter's Square. The Vatican did not issue comparative
figures on Thursday but figures released on January 4, 2013 showed
that some 2.3 million people attended all events presided by Benedict in
2012."

Pope Francis is perceived as a humble servant who refuses the
pomp and prestige of all of the popes before him. Wikipedia writes,
"Throughout his public life, both as an individual and as a religious
leader, Pope Francis has been noted for his humility, his concern for the
poor, and his commitment to dialogue as a way to build bridges between
people of all backgrounds, beliefs, and faiths. He is known for having a
simpler and less formal approach to the papacy, most notably by choosing
to reside in the Domus Sanctae Marthae guesthouse rather than the papal
apartments of the Apostolic Palace formerly used by his predecessors.
In addition, he is known for favoring simpler vestments void of
ornamentation, by starting to refuse the traditional papal mozzetta cape
upon his election, choosing silver instead of gold for his piscatorial ring,
and keeping the same pectoral cross he had when he was cardinal." [179]

Considering the Roman Catholic Church has always claimed that
there is no salvation outside of its institution, it has been interesting to
see how Pope Francis has embraced other religions and faiths. It is very
odd considering that Pope Benedict XVI had already reaffirmed on July
10, 2007 that that the Roman Catholic Church is the *one and only true
Church* and that "Orthodox Churches are defective, as well as, that other

---

[178] http://www.reuters.com/article/2014/01/02/us-pope-crowds-idUSBREA
0101720140102
[179] http://en.wikipedia.org/wiki/Jorge_Bergoglio

Christian denominations are not true Churches."[180] Prophecy scholars know that when there is a call for "unity" in the religious world that things are really heating up and the end time prophecies are coming to fulfillment. It is exciting yet tumultuous times! Remember God's warning to us in **1 Thessalonians 5:3**, where it says, **"For when they shall say, Peace and safety, then sudden destruction comes upon them, as travail upon a woman with child; and they shall not escape."**

This was the headline on March 20, 2013, *only a week* after Pope Francis' appointment to the papal throne: ***Pope urges religions, those with no Church to ally for justice.***[181] The article read, "Pope Francis urged members of all religions and those belonging to no church to unite to defend justice, peace and the environment and not allow the value of a person to be reduced to 'what he produces and what he consumes.' Yahya Pallavicini, a leader of Italy's Muslim community, said he was impressed by the pope's insistence of inter-religious friendship. Francis, elected a week ago as the first non-European pope in 1,300 years, met leaders of non-Catholic Christian religions such as Orthodox, Anglicans, Lutherans and Methodists, and others including Jews, Muslims, Buddhists and Hindus."

The article quoted Pope Francis stating to the religious leaders at the Vatican, "The Catholic Church is aware of the importance of furthering respect of friendship between men and women of different religious traditions." It went onto say, "Speaking in Italian in the frescoed Sala Clementina, he said members of all religions and even non-believers had to recognize their joint responsibility 'to our world, to all of creation, which we have to love and protect. We must do much for the good of the poorest, the weak, and those who are suffering, to favor justice, promote reconciliation and build peace,' he said. While he said history had shown that any attempt to eliminate God had produced 'much violence,' he reached out to those who seek truth, goodness and beauty without belonging to any religion. 'They are our precious allies in the commitment to defend human dignity, build a more peaceful coexistence among people and protect nature with care,' he said." While all of this

---

[180] http://www.msnbc.msn.com/id/19692094/

[181] http://www.reuters.com/article/2013/03/20/us-pope-idUSBRE92D05 P20130320

sounds just peachy, true believers know that the false way of religion is completely contrary to the salvation afforded once and for all by Jesus Christ on the Cross which paid the sin debt of mankind brought about by the Fall of Man. Pope Francis even says that atheists are redeemed in the following quote, "The Lord has redeemed all of us, all of us, with the Blood of Christ: all of us, not just Catholics. Everyone! 'Father, the atheists?' Even the atheists. Everyone! And this Blood makes us children of God of the first class! We are created children in the likeness of God and the Blood of Christ has redeemed us all! And we all have a duty to do good. And this commandment for everyone to do good, I think, is a beautiful path towards peace."[182]

The Church of Rome has murdered *millions* throughout the centuries for not accepting their false religion. Looking at Pope Francis' attitude toward different religions and faiths, it is contradictory to the teachings of Rome. There is a reason for this sudden shift and we will cover that in the next chapter. It completely lines up with prophecies of end time events written in the Bible! In the meantime let me state the belief of the Roman Catholic Church which has been upheld and reaffirmed since its inception. The Roman Catholic Church claims that salvation can only be administered by their religious institution. The *Catechism of the Catholic Church* states, "Basing itself on Scripture and Tradition, the Council teaches that the Church, a pilgrim now on earth, *is necessary for salvation* . . . Hence they could not be saved who, knowing that the Catholic Church was founded as necessary by God through Christ, would refuse either to enter it or to remain in it (my italics)."[183] The *St. Joseph's Annotated Catechism* states concerning salvation, "It is only through Christ's Catholic Church, which is 'the all-embracing means of salvation,' that one can benefit fully from the means of salvation."[184] However, **Acts 4:12** says, **"Neither is there Salvation in any other: for there is none other name under Heaven given among men, whereby we must be saved."** This name is *Jesus Christ*; not the Roman Catholic Church.

---

[182] http://www.chick.com/bc/2013/newpope.asp

[183] *Catechism of the Catholic Church*, Second Edition, 1997, paragraph 846

[184] *St. Joseph's Annotated Catechism*, Rev. Anthony Schraner, Catholic Book Publishing, New York, 1981, page 108-109 # 80 and 81

Even before Bergoglio's election, he was seen rubbing shoulders with those estranged from the Roman Catholic Church for centuries. One example is in November of 2012, where he brought leaders of the Jewish, Muslim, Evangelical and Orthodox faiths together in the Cathedral to pray for peace in the Middle East. In a 2013 Associated Press article it said that Bergoglio has a "very deep capacity for dialogue with other religions", and considers "healing divisions between religions a major part of the Catholic Church's mission."[185] Concerning the Orthodox Churches, which resulted from the Great Schism of 1054, Bergoglio has been recognized for his efforts "to further close the nearly 1,000-year estrangement with the Orthodox Churches." Antoni Sevruk, rector of the Russian Orthodox Church of Saint Catherine the Great Martyr in Rome, said that Bergoglio "often visited Orthodox services in the Russian Orthodox Annunciation Cathedral in Buenos Aires" and is known as an advocate on behalf the Orthodox Church in dealing with Argentina's government. Bergoglio's positive relationship with the Eastern Orthodox Churches is reflected in the fact that Patriarch Bartholomew I of Constantinople attended his papal installation. This is the first time since the Great Schism of 1054 that the Orthodox Ecumenical Patriarch of Constantinople, a position considered first among equals in the Eastern Orthodox Church organization, has attended a papal installation. Orthodox leaders state that Bartholomew's decision to attend the ceremony shows that the relationship between the Orthodox and Catholic Churches is a priority of his.[186]

Concerning Judaism, Bergoglio had close ties to the Jewish community of Argentina attending Rosh Hashanah services in 2007 at a synagogue in Buenos Aires. He told the Jewish congregation during his visit that he went to the synagogue to examine his heart, "like a pilgrim, together with you, my elder brothers."[187] The same source reveals that the leaders of the Islamic community in Buenos Aires welcomed the news of Bergoglio's election as pope, noting that he "always showed himself as a friend of the Islamic community", and a person whose position is "pro-dialogue."

---

[185] http://en.wikipedia.org/wiki/Jorge_Mario_Bergoglio
[186] http://en.wikipedia.org/wiki/Jorge_Mario_Bergoglio
[187] http://en.wikipedia.org/wiki/Jorge_Mario_Bergoglio

Shortly after Pope Francis' election, during a meeting with ambassadors from 180 countries accredited with the Holy See of Rome, Pope Francis called for more interreligious dialogue; particularly with Islam. He also expressed gratitude that so many civil and religious leaders from the Islamic world had attended his installation Mass.[188] He recognized that Muslims "worship the one living and merciful God, and call upon him in prayer."[189] This reaffirms Vatican II, where it was pronounced that Muslims worship the same "one true God." It specifically states, "The Church regards with esteem also the Muslims. They adore the one God, living and subsisting in himself; merciful and all-powerful, the Creator of heaven and earth, who has spoken to men; they take pains to submit wholeheartedly to even his inscrutable decrees, just as Abraham, with whom the faith of Islam takes pleasure in linking itself, submitted to God." True born again Christians know that we do not worship the same God as the Muslims do. Allah is the moon god and our God is Jehovah or Elohim, the Creator of the Universe!

Another important event which prophecy scholars are watching for is a peace treaty for Israel. There is so much interesting history with God's chosen people who were first called the Israelites. They are also known as the Hebrews or the Jews. This race of people began when God chose Abraham and promised him that the seed of the Redeemer would come through his bloodline. God told Abraham in **Genesis 15:5, "Look toward the Heaven, and tell the stars, if you be able to number them: and He said unto him, So shall your seed be."** At 100 years of age, Abraham and his 90 year old wife, Sarah, conceived a son, whom they named Isaac. Isaac married Rebekah and together they conceived twins, Esau and Jacob. Jacob, who was later named Israel by God, was given the birthright and from him the 12 Tribes of Israel were born. Jesus came specifically through the Tribe of Judah.

Unfortunately, the Jewish people did not accept Jesus as the Messiah whom God had sent to redeem them and the religious leaders under the control of the Roman Emperor crucified Him. **John 1:11 says, "He came unto His Own, and His Own received Him not."** The Jews

---

[188] http://en.wikipedia.org/wiki/Jorge_Mario_Bergoglio
[189] http://www.catholic.com/blog/todd-aglialoro/christians-muslims-and-the-one-god

shouted to crucify Jesus and in **Matthew 27:25** it records them saying in unison, "**. . . His blood be on us, and on our children.**" God has made many promises to the Jewish people because of their rejection of Jesus. **Isaiah 1:15** says, "**And when you spread forth your hands, I will hide My eyes from you: yea, when you make many prayers, I will not hear: your hands are full of blood.**" God knew that the Jews would be dispersed from their land and fiercely persecuted. God has allowed this to happen, but He has not forgotten His chosen people. He still fully intends to set up His Kingdom in the promised land of Jerusalem just as He has promised them thousands of years ago.

It says in **Deuteronomy 28: 63, 64, 65**, "**. . . and you shall be plucked from off the land where you go to possess it . . . And the LORD shall scatter you among all people, from one end of the Earth even unto the other . . . And among these nations shall you find no ease, neither shall the sole of your foot have rest . . .**" And in **Zechariah 7:14** it says, "**But I scattered them with a whirlwind among all the nations whom they knew not. Thus the land was desolate after them, that no man passed through nor returned: for they laid the pleasant land desolate.**" This has been very true of the Jewish people over the centuries and also true of the then barren land of Israel, which is the land God had promised them. The Jews were scattered all over the world without a homeland. Not only were these Jews never truly accepted by other countries, but they have also been persecuted mercilessly over the centuries. No other race of people could have managed to survive as a nation for over 2000 years; especially under the challenging conditions which the Jews have experienced. Not only have the Jewish people kept their nationality, they have also managed to keep the Hebrew language alive. This is truly remarkable and I believe it is an act of God!

The land of Israel was a desolate barren oasis, just as God promised, until very recently. Although some tried to make the land prosper, it just would not. **Zechariah 8:7** shows God promising the Israelites, "**Thus saith the LORD of Hosts; Behold, I will save My people from the east country, and from the west country; And I will bring them, and they shall dwell in the midst of Jerusalem . . .**" And **Jeremiah 31:10** says, "**. . . He who scatters Israel will gather him, and keep him, as a shepherd does his flock.**" Just as God had promised, in the year 1948,

Israel was made a nation again and the Jews began pouring back into their homeland. This land is now flourishing at an unbelievable rate; producing and exporting produce which was thought could never have grown on its barren soil!

The fight to obtain ownership of Israel, and especially the Holy Land of Jerusalem, has always been a struggle. The Bible calls her, **"a cup of trembling (Zechariah 12:2)."** There is so much history and monumental future events which will take place in Jerusalem and the Holy Land has always been the apple of the Vatican's eye! Ignatius Loyola and all successive Jesuit Generals have continually tried to establish the Order's base of operation in Jerusalem. From Bible prophecy, we know that Antichrist will bring a seven year peace agreement and will allow the rebuilding of Solomon's Temple which was destroyed for the second time in 70 A.D. by the Roman General Titus. The rebuilding of Solomon's Temple has been in the works for decades now and *The Temple Institute* in Jerusalem has already created much of the furniture of the Temple, the priestly garments and has even begun training boys and men of the Tribe of Levi to be the priests in charge of the Temple and the future sacrifices.[190] From what I understand, the Temple could be built very quickly because the preparations have all been made. The Jews are only waiting for their spot to open on the Temple Mount where the third most holy site of Islam stands today, the Dome of the Rock. This site is where Muslims believe that Muhammad was taken up to Heaven. Many and most believe that Antichrist will be the man who will make it possible for the Jews to rebuild their Temple either here or some believe that they will build it side by side with the Dome of the Rock.

Here is a little inside information from an article called "Pope's Temple Mount" which reveals how the Vatican was deeded the Temple Mount in Jerusalem in 1993: "The institution of 'The Vatican' is not understood by Israelis and Jews . . . Thus, a secret deal could be done between the Vatican and the State of Israel and nobody in Israel would ever find out about it. In fact, that is exactly what happened . . . First, you have to realize that for centuries the Vatican has attempted to obtain control of Jerusalem, which started with the Crusades. For

---

[190] http://www.templeinstitute.org/main.htm

them to convince the world that the Messiah [the Antichrist] they intend to put on the world's stage is going to be accepted as genuine, they need to perform this play in the Old City [Jerusalem]. The story of this production is that this 'Messiah' will merge the three monotheistic religions [Christianity (most of who are really Roman Catholics), Islam and Judaism], usher in peace and harmony in the world, and solve the Middle East conflict . . . The 'Chronology of Events' for the Vatican's conquest of the Old City of Jerusalem is as follows:"

- On October 12th, 1991, the head of the World Jewish Congress, [Member of the CFR] Edgar Bronfman, is appointed head of the International Jewish Committee of Inter-religious Consultation to conduct official contact with the Vatican and the State of Israel.
- On March 17th, 1992, Jerusalem Mayor [a Freemason] Teddy Kollek says: 'The Israeli government should meet the Vatican's demand to apply special status for Jerusalem.
- On April 15th, 1992, Cardinal Joseph Ratzinger [who became Pope Benedict XVI] visits Israel for the first time but only meets with Jerusalem Mayor Teddy Kollek.
- The story of the Catholic Church's attempt to abscond with the Old City of Jerusalem from the Jews begins in July, 1992 . . . literally from the moment the new Rabin-led Labor government took over from Yitzhak Shamir's defeated Likud party, secret talks between the Vatican and the State of Israel began. What precipitated these secret talks?
- On September 10, 1993, just three days before the signing of the Oslo Accords in Washington, the Italian newspaper *La Stampa* reported that then *Foreign Minister Shimon Peres* [a Freemason] *concluded a secret deal with the Vatican to hand over sovereignty of Jerusalem's Old City to the Vatican.* The agreement was included in the secret clauses of the 'Declaration of Principles' signed on September 13th, 1993, in Washington, D.C.
- In the same week that Israeli Foreign Minister and chief Oslo architect Shimon Peres signed the 'Declaration of Principles' with Yasser Arafat in Washington, the Israeli-Vatican commission held a special meeting in Israel. Under the Vatican agreement, the Israelis would give over control of the Old City to the Vatican

before the year 2000. The plan also calls for Jerusalem to become the second Vatican of the world with all three major religions represented, but under the authority of the Vatican. Jerusalem will remain the capital of Israel but the Old City will be administered by the Vatican.

- In May, 1994, Mark Halter, a French intellectual and philosopher and a close friend of Peres, tells the Israeli weekly magazine *HaShishi* that he personally delivered a letter from Peres to the Pope in September, 1993, in which Peres promised to internationalize Jerusalem, granting the UN political control of the Old City of Jerusalem, and [granting] the Vatican hegemony of the holy sites within. The UN would give the PLO a capital within its new territory and East Jerusalem would become a kind of free trade zone of world diplomacy.

- In March, 1995, a cable from the Israeli Embassy in Rome to the Foreign Ministry in Jerusalem is leaked to radio station *Arutz Sheva*, confirming the handover of Jerusalem to the Vatican. Two days later the cable made the front page of *Haaretz*.

- In April, 1995, Knesset Member Avraham Shapira announced in the Knesset that he had information that all Vatican property in Jerusalem was to become tax exempt and that large tracts of real estate on Mount Zion [the Temple Mount] were given to the pope in perpetuity.

- In March, 2000, the pope visits the Holy Land and repeats the Holy See's [the Vatican] insistence that 'international oversight—a special statute, internationally guaranteed—would best safeguard the city's holy sites and all its religions' [all of which is in preparation for the future Antichrist's confirming of an international "peace covenant" with Jerusalem **(Isaiah 28:15, 18; Daniel 9:27)].**"[191]

This is a long article, but I did not want to leave out these important dated details. To summarize this article, Israel's Foreign Minister Shimon Peres deeded the Temple Mount to the papacy in 1993 and "concluded a secret deal with the Vatican to hand over the sovereignty of Jerusalem's

---

[191] *Temple Mount, "Third Article: The Vatican Agenda,"* Barry Chamish and Anonymous Contributor, (2003) pp. 3, 4, 5, 6, 7, 8, 9.

Old City to the Vatican!" Although the Temple has yet to be rebuilt as of today, this was a major milestone for the Vatican and the Jesuit General.

How instrumental could the present pope be in this future peace treaty for Israel? Here is an excerpt from an article in *Bloomberg,* dated January 14, 2014 titled, *Kerry Seeks Pope Francis's Support for Mideast Peace Push.* "U.S. Secretary of State John Kerry is looking to Pope Francis, spiritual leader of the world's 1.2 billion Roman Catholics, for help in his efforts to negotiate peace between Muslims and Jews. In a visit to the Vatican today, Kerry met with the Holy See's top diplomat, Secretary of State Pietro Parolin, to discuss Mideast developments and other matters, including the agenda for a planned meeting between President Barack Obama and the new pope . . . They discussed Israel-Palestinian peace talks in preparation for the pope's announced visit to Israel, Jordan and the Palestinian territories in May . . . In a statement, the Vatican said Kerry met with Archbishop Parolin for an hour and 40 minutes, discussing 'the peace process in the Middle East, especially the situation in Syria and the preparations for the Geneva II Middle East Peace Conference, and negotiations between Israel and Palestine.'" Kerry said, "Obviously, there are issues of enormous concern to the Holy See, not just about peace, but also about the freedom of access for religious worship in Jerusalem for all religions"[192] Will Pope Francis help to move forward with a peace treaty? Only time will tell!

It may seem vindictive to be discussing Pope Francis in such a negative way when by all accounts, he seems to be a humble peace-seeking pope. But please remember some very pertinent facts. One being that this man, Jorge Bergoglio, took the deadly Jesuit Oath which was the most shocking and disheartening words that ever passed before my eyes. We are speaking about a man who swore to secretly *"act as a dissembler"* and a man that has *"been taught to insidiously plant the seeds of jealousy and hatred between communities, provinces, states that were at peace, and incite them to deeds of blood, involving them in war with each other, and to create revolutions and civil wars in countries that were independent and prosperous . . ."* What about the portion of Bergoglio's oath where he says, *"I furthermore promise and declare that I will, when opportunity*

---

[192] http://www.bloomberg.com/news/2014-01-14/kerry-seeks-pope-francis-s-support-for-mideast-peace-push.html

present, make and wage relentless war, secretly or openly, against all heretics, Protestants and Liberals, as I am directed to do, to extirpate and exterminate them from the face of the whole earth; and that I will spare neither age, sex or condition; and that I will hang, waste, boil, flay, strangle and bury alive these infamous heretics, rip up the stomachs and wombs of their women and crush their infants' heads against the walls, in order to annihilate forever their execrable race. That when the same cannot be done openly, I will secretly use the poisoned cup, the strangulating cord, the steel of the poniard or the leaden bullet, regardless of the honor, rank, dignity, or authority of the person or persons, whatever may be their condition in life, either public or private, as I at any time may be directed so to do by any agent of the Pope or Superior of the Brotherhood of the Holy Faith, of the Society of Jesus."193

Maybe that is why I personally get extremely agitated when I read Pope Francis statements such as, "Wars shatter and hurt so many lives! Their most vulnerable victims were children, elderly, battered women and the sick."[194] He should get an Oscar this year for best actor! The cameras always seem to capture him doing some marvelous humble deed and the pictures are splattered all over Facebook, Twitter and the Jesuit biased news. One article posted on December 16, 2013 really got my goat. It was titled, ***"I Knew Pope Francis Was Good, But When I Found Out Everything He Did in 2013, I Was Blown Away."*** If the world did not already think that this man could practically walk on water, then this article would certainly convince them that he could. Some highlights were photos and captions such as: He invited a boy with Down's Syndrome for a ride in the "pope mobile"; Pope Francis embraced Vinicio Riva, a man scarred by a genetic disease; Pope Francis has stated several times that the Church has no right to interfere spiritually in the lives of gays and lesbians, which led *The Advocate*, a gay rights magazine, to name Francis the 'single most influential person of 2013 on the lives of LGBT people'; The pope held a major Holy Week service at Casal del Marmo jail for minors, rather than the Vatican. During the service, the pope washed and kissed the feet of 12 young offenders to commemorate Jesus' gesture of humility towards his apostles on the night before he died. During the service, he broke tradition by washing the feet of women

---

[193] http://www.reformation.org/jesuit-oath.html
[194] http://www.reuters.com/article/2013/12/25/us-pope-christmas-idUSBRE9BN0MA20131225

and Muslims; It has been discovered that Pope Francis regularly leaves the Vatican at night to feed the homeless; Francis donated his own Harley Davidson motorcycle to fund a hostel and soup kitchen in Rome; Francis paid respect to the end of Ramadan. He stated that both Christians and Muslims worship the same God, and he hoped that Christians and Muslims would work together to promote mutual respect; Pope Francis invited a group of homeless men and their dog into the Vatican to share his birthday meal along with his staff. The pope had decided that he wanted a small birthday event, which would do some good, rather than a large and expensive event.

Let us look at the significance of Jorge Bergoglio choosing the papal name of "Francis I." This name was chosen on honor of Francis of Assisi, who called for reform within the Roman Catholic Church and created the Franciscan Order in the year of 1209. What is so very interesting is that Order of the Franciscans were chief among the inquisitors of the famous Roman Catholic Inquisitions which in totality has killed millions upon millions of so-called "heretics." Basically a "heretic" was viewed as anyone who did not accept the teachings of Rome. Seeing the mountain of evidence which this manuscript has laid out, and knowing that the Roman Catholic Church, via the Jesuits, is planning the largest inquisition ever conceived, don't you think it is very remarkable that Jorge Bergoglio would be the first to take the name of Francis? Did you know that Pope Francis called born again believers, "Right wing Christian fundamentalist" and said that it was an "illness."[195] These are the people who believe the Bible, and believe that salvation is through the blood of Jesus Christ alone. We are seen as intolerant because of our firm stand on God's Word as the yardstick for truth.

The Bible talks very plainly in the Book of Revelation about a "false prophet," who will be Antichrist's right hand man and chief promoter. It says in **Revelation 13:11-12, "And I beheld another beast coming up out of the earth; and he had two horns like a lamb, and he spake as a dragon. And he exerciseth all the power of the first beast before him, and causeth the earth and them which dwell therein to worship the first beast, whose deadly wound was healed."** The lamb

---

like appearance is intended to deceive. The word **"dragon"** in the Bible denotes satanically inspired evil and it says here that the false prophet will speak as a dragon. Remember that in **Daniel 11:21**, it says of Antichrist, **"And in his estate shall stand up a vile person, to whom they shall not give the honour of the kingdom: but he shall come in peaceably, and obtain the kingdom by flatteries."** Putting all of this together, we know that Antichrist and the false prophet will bring about a false peace which much of the world will be deceived into believing to be true. But also, this "peace" will come to an end and Antichrist will set himself up to be worshipped as a god. No one will be able to buy or sell unless they receive his "mark," which is referred to as "the Mark of the Beast **(Revelation 13:16-18)**." This will be the ultimate "power trip!" And those who have not heeded the warnings in this book may be doomed to the oppressive control of Antichrist. Some will laugh, some will mock, but this is based on history, facts and prophecy, which is vastly becoming a reality.

Taking everything into consideration, I do firmly believe that the pope of Rome could very well be the "false prophet" mentioned in the Book of Revelation. Here is some further insight from the *Cutting Edge Ministries* website which explains the future scenario very well: "On the global scale, we have known since August 18, 1991, that the Illuminati *(created by Jesuit Adam Weishaupt)* had decided that the Roman Catholic pope—whomever he is at the time—will be the head religious figure of the global New World Order religion. This designation places the Pontiff as the False Prophet of Revelation 13:11-18. As False Prophet, the pope will unite all religions under his leadership, support Antichrist fully, display the same occult powers as Antichrist, and force the peoples of the world to take the Mark of the Beast (my comment in italics)."[196]

But who will be the Antichrist? This man will literally be empowered by Satan and in the second half of the Great Tribulation; the Bible says that Satan will literally indwell this man. Now, I am speculating here because no one can know who Antichrist will be. Because of the fact that the Jesuit General, the "Black Pope," and the pope of Rome, the "White Pope," are already working together to create this New World Order and

---

[196] http://www.cuttingedge.org/News/n2020.cfm

as stated above, it is possible that the "White Pope" may fit the bill as the false prophet figure; could it be possible that the Antichrist will be a "Black Pope?" Many will dismiss this possibility so let me explain myself further. Most Bible scholars will tell you that Antichrist will have to be of Jewish descent because the Jewish people will accept him as their Messiah and their long awaited Saviour. Remember that the Jews do not believe that Jesus Christ was the Saviour of mankind, and therefore, they called for His crucifixion! They are, however, awaiting a Messiah. Remember Jesus said in **John 5:43, "I am come in My Father's Name, and you receive me not: if another shall come in his own name, him you will receive."** Well, who is to say that the "Black Pope" will not be of Jewish blood? Many popes and leaders had Jewish blood, including Adolf Hitler![197] As a matter of fact, Ignatius Loyola, the first Jesuit General, was of Jewish descent.

Another reason which causes me to question whether the "Black Pope" could be the Antichrist is because we know that he is really the one running the show with the "White Pope" as the public figurehead. Up until the most recent papal election of Pope Francis, the Black Pope and the White Pope have despised one another. The Jesuits were seen as a threat and even suppressed on more than one occasion. In the past, the popes of Rome knew that their entire empires would crumble without the genius of the Jesuit Generals. That is why the appointment of Jesuit Jorge Bergoglio as Pope Francis I was such a *pivotal event*! Finally, the Jesuits have secured the most powerful public throne in the world and things will be moving very rapidly toward the destruction of the United States as a nation and the appearance of a New World Order under a fascist dictator, Antichrist.

Furthermore, the Bible says in **Revelation 17:16, "And the ten horns which you saw upon the beast, these shall hate the whore** (The universal religious system under the false prophet)**, and shall make her desolate and naked, and shall eat her flesh, and burn her with fire."** The ten horns represent the ten nation confederations under the rule of Antichrist. These ten nations will turn on **"the whore"** and burn her with fire. I think we will see more and more that Pope Francis will

197   http://www.lloydthomas.org/1-IsraelTimeLine/7-1930-1999/hitler.html

slowly begin moving away from traditional Roman Catholic doctrines and we may even possibly see the Roman Catholic Church exposed in more scandal and humiliation. Satan has used this powerful religion to position his men precisely where he wants them, but he will ultimately have no use for her in the end.

A former bishop, high-ranking Vatican official and assistant to Pope John Paul II, by the name of Gerard Bouffard said, "I know firsthand that the Vatican controls and monitors everything in Israel with the intention of destroying the Jews. The true purpose of the Jesuit Order is to orchestrate and control all leaders of the world in order to bring about a major worldwide conflict which will eventually destroy America, the Middle East and Israel. They destroy everything from within and *want to bring about the destruction of the Catholic Church*, as well, in order to usher in a one world religion based on Satanism (my italics)."[198]

So, we can see here that the root of all of this is the desire of Satan to have the people of the world to worship him instead of Jehovah God. We can point fingers to who will be this or that figure described in the Bible, but the absolute bottom line is that *Satan wants to rule the world*! He will have his way for a short time, but the Bible describes his ultimate fate in **Revelation 20:10**, where it says, **"And the Devil who deceived them was cast into the Lake of Fire and brimstone, where the Beast and the False Prophet are, and shall be tormented day and night forever and ever."** The Bible has been 100% accurate so far and His Word will not alter what has already been written. **"I am the Lord and I change not (Malachi 3:6)."**

---

[198] http://www.spirittruth.com/view/?pageID=73185

Chapter Eleven

OVERWHELMING EVIDENCE

If we could view this next chapter as a court trial, with the papacy of the Roman Catholic Church and the Jesuits as the accused and the reader as a juror, how would one find the defendant: guilty or not guilty? Just to be fair, let us briefly lay out the evidence again so that one can make a justified verdict in this case. I truly believe that by using history and by looking at the terrible condition which the United States of America is in presently, the case is solid against the accused, but I do not want to sway anyone's decision. I am sure if the Vatican would have a chance to plead her case, she would most definitely try to sell us on the phrase, "But . . . we have *changed!*" I would personally love more than anything to believe that, but the facts are the facts and covering up the intentions of Jesuits to have world domination by "any means necessary," really make it hard to believe that the Roman Catholic Church, being run by the Jesuit Order, has truly changed.

Knowing that Satan is behind this push for a one world dictator, Antichrist, who will *literally* be satanically inspired, let us look at the hand of Satan in the conditions of the world we live in today. He was the one who came in the form of a serpent into the beautiful Garden of Eden and brought sin and death into God's perfect world by corrupting Adam, thereby causing the Fall of Man **(Genesis 3:1-24)**. Even though God promised a Redeemer and gave man a second chance, it did not stop

Satan from trying to set himself up as the god of this world which is his ultimate desire. The Bible actually refers to him as **"The prince of the Earth (John 12:31)"** because of the fact that he has dominion over man until the person is "born-again" by accepting the price that Jesus Christ paid for him at Calvary.

The world became so corrupt after Adam and Eve fell that God destroyed the Earth with a flood and everyone inhabiting it saving only Noah and his family. Once the Earth began being repopulated, it was not long before Satan's magnum opus, the Tower of Babel, became the original site of paganism with sun worship under the mighty Nimrod, who came to be known as "Baal." Of course, God confounded the languages of the people and they were dispersed all over the world carrying their pagan worship practices with them. Egypt became the world's super power and the powerful Egyptian Pharaohs continued to practice sun worship. Egypt was defeated by Syria, which was in turn overtaken by the Roman Empire, ruled by the Emperor or Caesar. This is the same empire which was in control when Jesus, came over 2000 years ago. Jesus was born during the oppressive rule of Rome and was crucified on a Roman cross. He died and was resurrected as the Saviour of all of mankind.

After Jesus' death, resurrection and ascension into Heaven, His Disciples began fulfilling the Great Commission and preached the Gospel, but because the early Church was severely persecuted by the Romans and the religious Jews, the Gospel made its way to many other areas of the world. The Roman Emperor Constantine issued the Edict of Milan in 313 A.D. which made Rome neutral in regards to worship and then he set himself up as the leader of this new pagan universal Church which came to be known as the Roman Catholic Church. Before this time, the Roman Empire was just a controlling government force under the leadership of the Emperor, but by adding religion, they became the spiritual and temporal ruling power on Earth. But remember, that in 331 A.D. Constantine issued another edict that those who had not come under the authority of Rome would be arrested, persecuted and their Churches and Church records were to be burned.

The Roman Catholic Church gained a great abundance of wealth and power and subordinated all of the kings of the Earth and all of the people with her religious system because she boastfully claimed that there was no salvation outside of her institution. She forbid the people to read God's Word and therefore the Dark Ages began followed by crusades, massacres and inquisitions which killed millions upon millions of Christians, Jews and others who would not bow down to her religious system set forth.

The Reformation began under Martin Luther which caused many Roman Catholics to see "Mother Church" as she really was: an oppressive ruler! As a result, many people were set free from the stronghold of Rome, but were branded as "Protestants" by Pope Paul III. The Counter Reformation led by Ignatius Loyola, who created the Jesuit Order, rose to power and attempted to gain back the spiritual and temporal power for the papacy. Combined with the Council of Trent and the Papal Inquisitions, the Jesuits worked diligently to regain control for the Church of Rome "by any means necessary."

The Protestants grew weary of persecution and set out to find a new land where they could be free from harassment and from the threat of the deadly Roman Catholic inquisitions. The Jesuits followed in disguise and planted Roman Catholics posing as Protestants all over the New World to infiltrate and destroy everything the Protestants were building. The United States became a nation in 1776, the same year that Jesuit Adam Weishaupt began the Order of the Illuminati, where the goals were identical to that of the Jesuit Order. In 1790, *Rome, Maryland* becomes our nation's capital and was renamed Washington D.C. by Jesuit trained Daniel Carroll. Incidentally, his Jesuit brother, John Carroll became the first bishop in America and founded the oldest Jesuit University in America, Georgetown University in Washington D.C.

In 1882, the Knights of Columbus, an American Catholic fraternity, came into existence to be the strong arm of the pope here in America. Their collective goal has been to "make America Catholic," and to work diligently to secure political positions. Also, in the late 1800's and early 1900's, there was a push for a unified world government by Jesuit trained Cecil Rhodes as well as a plan to deliberately launch a "social gospel" into the mainline denominations which would water down the true message of the Bible.

Jesuit Pierre Teilhard de Chardin then created the New Age Movement which combined with Humanistic Psychology and the new social gospel being preached made way for the "Seeker Sensitive Churches," "Purpose Driven Churches" and "Emerging Churches" which are so prevalent all over the United States presently. God warned us in **Matthew 13:25** that the enemy would come in and **"sow tares among the wheat."** Remember that the symptoms of consuming the false wheat would be apathetic, dim sighted people with an inability to walk. Well, Humanistic Psychology, the New Age Movement and the modern Seeker Sensitive Church movements, such as the Purpose Driven Church movement and the Emerging Church movement have done exactly that to the Church world as we know it today. For one, the New Age movement was introduced by a Jesuit and the "contemplative prayer" or meditation techniques mimic Ignatius Loyola's *Spiritual Exercises* which each Jesuit initiate must master. These *Spiritual Exercises* are what makes a Jesuit so completely empty of themselves so that they can do whatever it is that their Jesuit superiors call them to do. Part of the initiation process includes the Jesuit to state that he took an oath "to destroy heretics and their governments and rulers. And to spare neither age, sex nor condition. *To be as a corpse*, without any opinion or will of my own, but to implicitly obey my Superiors in all things without hesitation of murmuring (my italics)."

The Purpose Driven promoter, Rick Warren, was mentored by Peter Drucker who stated that, "Warren is not building a tent revival ministry, like the old-style evangelist, he is building an army, like the Jesuits." Rick Warren obviously admires Loyola and was proud to post a quote from Ignatius Loyola on his Twitter account recently which said, ""The servant of God earns half a doctorate through illness."[199] Also, to reiterate, Rick Warren is a member of the Council on Foreign Relations which is a Jesuit founded and controlled organization. Almost all directors and seats on the CFR are Roman Catholic Jesuit trained individuals. Why would a so-called Baptist Pastor align himself with such an organization? And as

---

[199] https://twitter.com/RickWarren/status/6818904517

for the Emergent Church Movement, it was endorsed by Peter Drucker as well. The Emerging Church also promotes Roman Catholic traditions such as Advent, Lent, Stations of the Cross and more.

More evidence toward the case against the Jesuits and the Roman Catholic Church is that the Vatican is responsible for the Ecumenical Movement which was introduced during the Vatican II Council of 1962. The purpose of this Ecumenical Movement was to blur the lines between true Biblical Christianity and Roman Catholicism. This movement has greatly damaged the Reformation of the 1500s. This is when Roman Catholics began to call themselves "Christians." And then in 1986, Pope John Paul II invited 160 religious leaders from 12 major religions to St. Peter's Basilica for prayer claiming that they were all praying to the same god. Then, of course, in 1994, they created the "Evangelicals and Catholics together: the Christian Mission in the Third Millennium." All of these were seemingly genuine outreaches to the Protestants, who through the centuries had been murdered through the various Roman Catholic inquisitions.

Through careful maneuvering, the Jesuits set up the Federal Reserve in 1913 as a money machine to fund their various activities including several wars. Having control of the financial aspect of the United States put them in a very significant position. They would slowly work on bankrupting the nation through war, shady financial deals on Wall Street and even eventually shift the trade market to countries outside of the United States. What once was a prosperous nation has become a destitute embarrassed nation with its tail between its legs while the national debt literally grows each millisecond! We are talking about currently being *trillions* of dollars in debt! Our founding fathers fought against a central bank and warned us that the implementation of such would cause us to self-destruct! Remember Thomas Jefferson's appeal? He said, "The central bank is an institution of the most deadly hostility existing against the principles and form of our Constitution . . . If the American people allow private banks to control the issuance of their currency, first by inflation and then by deflation, the banks and corporations that will grow up around them will deprive the people of all their property until their children will wake up homeless on the continent their fathers conquered."[200] What a sad state of affairs because this is precisely what is happening presently.

By utilizing immigration, the Jesuits promised to secure the majority in the United States so that the votes of the Roman Catholics would overpower the country. Remember the malicious promise given by the Jesuits in Charles Chiniquy's book, *Fifty Years in the Church of Rome?* "Silently and patiently, we must mass our Roman Catholics in the great cities of the United States, remembering that the vote of a poor journeyman, though he be covered with rags, has as much weight in the scale of powers as the millionaire Astor, and that if we have two votes against his one, he will become as powerless as an oyster. *Let us then multiply our votes;* let us call our poor but faithful Irish Catholics from every corner of the world, and gather them into the very hearts of the cities of Washington, New York, Boston, Chicago, Buffalo, Albany, Troy, Cincinnati . . . Let no one awake those sleeping lions, today. *Let us pray God that they continue to sleep a few years longer, waking only to find their votes outnumbered as we will turn them forever, out of every position of honor, power and profit!* . . . What will those so-called giants think when not a single senator or member of Congress will be chosen, unless he has submitted to our holy father the Pope! *We will not only elect the president, but fill and command the armies, man the navies, and hold the keys of the public treasury* . . . Then, yes! Then, we will rule the United States and lay them at the feet of the Vicar of Jesus Christ, that he may put an end to their godless system of education and impious laws of liberty of conscience, which are an insult to God and man (my italics)!"[201] This promise most definitely should be added to our mounting evidence against the accused party!

Also please remember Cardinal Roger Mahony who fights for illegal immigration, even forming "cities of sanctuary" for these illegals and encouraging priests to defy immigration laws! The frustration that most citizens feel with our government today stems from the Jesuits attempt to gain control of the country. The people holding the political seats and making the decisions that affect our country are majority Roman Catholics!

---

[200] http://www.phnet.fi/public/mamaa1/jefferson.htm
[201] *Fifty Years in the Church of Rome*, Charles Chiniquy, Chick Publications, pages 281,282

Not to mention that they have taken complete control of our armed forces and are moving quickly to gain control over local police forces. This is paramount to affectively enforce martial law once the plan is set.

Let us also not forget the quest of the Jesuits to control and destroy our education system here in the United States. I present again Justin Fulton's warning given in 1888 in his manuscript titled *Washington in the Lap of Rome*: "The United States has established schools, where they invite the people to send their children, that they may cultivate their intelligence and become good and useful citizens. The Church of Rome has publicly cursed all these schools and forbidden their children to attend them, under pain of excommunication in this world and damnation in the next. Not only does she antagonize our school system, claiming at the outset that it bore a religious character, because the Bible found in it a welcome; but having been the cause for banishing the Word of God, she pronounces the schools godless, and sends forth the decree to have all her children housed in the parochial school, and then, with an effrontery and inconsistency that is simply astounding, she seeks to officer the schools of Protestants, so that in some of the public schools in which there is hardly a single Roman Catholic child, and where there is a parochial school in the immediate neighborhood, Rome, through suffrage obtains control of the School Board in our large cities, and then fills the schools with Roman Catholic teachers to instruct the children of Protestants. In one such school are forty-one teachers, thirty-nine of whom are Roman Catholics." Fulton also says that the Jesuits saw that "Romanism is doomed if the people of this land are to be educated . . . they understand that they are to secure the control of this continent, by destroying the public school system of America."[202]

Along with the annihilation of the education system, it was important for the Jesuits to destroy the credibility of the Bible and to get it out of the hands of the people. The Bible was the weapon of choice used by the Reformers and although the Roman Catholic Church forbid her faithful followers to read the Word of God, it was still God ordained that many brave men would work till their death to have the Bible available to the "common people." All of these men were punished greatly for their courageousness and lost their lives by the hand of Rome. Here again is

---

[202] *Washington in the Lap of Rome*, Justin Fulton, Hard Press Publishing, 1888, pages 47-48

the quote from the *New Advent Catholic Encyclopedia* online, under the term "Protestantism:" "The supremacy of the Bible as source of faith is unhistorical, ill logical, fatal to the virtue of faith, and destructive of unity." How very sad that they view the Bible in this light! The Jesuits also spoke spitefully of the Bible when they were quoted saying, "Then the Bible, that serpent which, with head erect and eyes flashing fire, threatens us with its venom whilst it trails along the ground, shall be changed again into a rod as soon as we are able to seize it; For you know but too well that, for three centuries past, this cruel asp has left us no repose; you well know with what folds it entwines us, and with what fangs it gnaws us."[203] Please remember that Roman Catholic Rupert Murdoch's ownership over Harper Collins Publishing makes it possible for the Roman Catholic Church to have the legal copyright to all newer Bible versions! All of the new Bible versions (NIV, NASV, etc.) are based not on the original manuscript from which the *King James Version Bible* was derived, the *Textus Receptus*, but on the two so-called "ancient" manuscripts found in the custody of the Roman Catholic Church: The *Codex Sinaiticus* and the *Codex Vaticanus* which have many thousands of errors and have been proven to be forgeries.

The Jesuits again have obtained control of the mainstream media, whether it be television, or print. This is of extreme importance because they consider themselves to be social engineers and therefore, "engineers of the soul." Through the media, they can brainwash the American public. John Wylie said, "There are two institutions in special to which the Jesuits will lay siege. These are the press and the pulpit . . ."[204] Here is a bold confession made by John Swinton, the Chief of Staff for the *New York Times* in 1953 at the New York Press Club: "There is no such thing, at this date of the world's history, in America, as an independent press. You know it, and I know it. There is not one of you who dares to write your honest opinions, and if you did, you know beforehand that it would never appear in print. I am paid weekly for *keeping my honest opinion out of the paper* I am connected with. Others of you are paid similar salaries for similar things, and any of you who would be so foolish as to write

---

[203] *The Jesuit Conspiracy: The Secret Plan of the Order*, Abate Leone, Chapman and Hall, 1848, page 98

[204] *The Jesuits: Their Morals, Maxims and Plots against Kings, Nations and Churches.* By J. A. Wylie Pages 93 - 94

honest opinions would be out on the streets looking for another job. If I allowed my honest opinions to appear in one issue of my newspaper, before twenty-four hours my occupation would be gone. *The business of the journalists is to destroy the truth; to lie outright; to pervert; to vilify; to fawn at the feet of mammon, and to sell his country and his race for his daily bread. You know it, and I know it and what folly is this toasting an independent press? We are the tools and vassals of rich men behind the scenes. We are the jumping jacks, they pull the strings and we dance. Our talents, our possibilities and our lives are all the property of other men. We are intellectual prostitutes* (my italics)."[205]

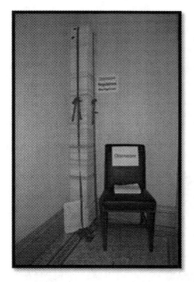

Another important topic which was just barely covered in this manuscript is the big picture of the healthcare within the United States of America. We did touch very briefly on Obamacare, also termed the "Affordable Care Act" which was recently passed. The original Obamacare legislation was 2,700 pages and was given to legislators less than 24 hours before they were to vote on it, which made it humanly impossible to read the entire document and adequately vote. If that was not bad enough, the Obamacare regulations have since grown to over 20,000 pages and stand a whopping 7 feet 3 inches tall! Healthcare in the United States is very important in the takeover plan by Satan's Jesuit Order. This too has been in the works for well over a hundred years. In 1888, Justin Fulton writes, "Is it a surprising fact, that every hospital in Washington is in the hands of Roman Catholics . . ."[206] The "Sisters of Mercy," which are Roman Catholic nuns, ran the hospitals at this time and there were countless stories of Protestants being denied care. These Protestants were "heretics" in their eyes, so it was doing the Church of Rome a great service by allowing them to die. The Reverend J.W. Parker of E-Street

[205] Multiple contributors, A U.S. Police Action: Operation Vampire Killer, The American Citizens and Laumen Association, pp. 18,19,
[206] *Washington in the Lap of Rome*, Justin Fulton, Hardpress Publishing, 1888, page 87

Baptist Church of Washington, D.C. related that his own brother was in a Washington hospital where the nuns were the nurses and he had asked for a drink of water in the night. He overheard the nun say, "He is a heretic; let him choke." There are other horror stories of those who were treated worse than a stray dog in the hospitals of Washington. Could it be that Obamacare will discriminate care for those who do not agree with the "standard" belief system set forth?

In reviewing the evidence, we must once again visit the FEMA detention camps which are planted all over the United States. These are refurbished abandoned railroad stations, military and industrial complexes to be used and I have even read about the use of large sports facilities and Walmart stores agreeing to be used as FEMA camps.[207] With the *National Defense Authorization Act* recently pushed through, the imprisonment of American citizens is a reality! Remember that the NDAA legalizes arresting American citizens and holding them for an indefinite amount of time without a trial or explanation. We have also seen that there are hundreds of thousands of plastic coffins, which can easily fit a family of four if needed, being stored all over the United States. And to further drive home the imminent threat, the local police forces are purchasing military grade vehicles and teaming with the military to help detain people. It is a little known fact that each and every one of us have a file in Rome that contains all of our personal information. Abbot M Leone said, "There are in the central house, at Rome, huge registers, wherein are inscribed the names of . . . all the important persons, friends, or enemies . . . It is the most gigantic biographical collection that has ever been formed . . . When it is required to act in any way upon an individual, they open the book and become immediately acquainted with his life, his character, his qualities, his defects, his projects, his family, his friends, his most secret acquaintances."[208] The "Data Mining" projected as a part of the "Common Core" curriculum requires unbelievably massive buildings, as well, to store the data which will be obtained from the children involved.

Please also recall the massive amounts of ammunition which the Department of Homeland Security has purchased recently. Just to refresh

---

[207] http://thecommonsenseshow.com/2014/01/30/all-major-league-sports-facilities-are-the-new-fema-camps/

[208] *Codeword Barbelon*, P.D. Stuart, Lux-Verbi Books, 2009, page 13

our memories, it was confirmed that besides the already 1.6 *billion* rounds of ammunition purchased in just ten months' time, the DHS also purchased another 21.6 million rounds and that the war on Iraq used only approximately 70 million rounds per year. [209] The DHS was created after the 9/11 disaster and its job description is that it works in the civilian sphere to protect the United States within and also the outside borders. The stated goal is to prepare for, prevent, and respond to domestic emergencies, particularly terrorism. This organization is not to be confused with the Department of Defense which is responsible for military actions abroad. [210] Now differentiating between the Department of Homeland Security and the Department of Defense makes you wonder why the DHS would need *that* much ammunition! Also, according to the DHS insider source quoted in an earlier chapter, he reveals that "preparations have been finalized to respond to a crisis of unprecedented magnitude within the United States. The response will include the use of lethal force against U.S. citizens under the instructions of Barack Obama." He suggests the fact that it may be a result of the snowballing effects of an economic collapse where the American people will not be able to use ATM cards or retrieve money out of the banks. He goes on to say that this will be a deliberate and planned collapse of the economy but the citizens will not be aware of that fact.

To further add to the suspicion, in the last few weeks as of February 2014, there has been a rash of banker "suicides" where bankers are supposedly jumping to their deaths, killing themselves in mysterious ways or just disappearing without a trace. One source writes, "Although the trail of mysterious and bizarre deaths . . . begin in late January, 2014, there are others. Not only that, *there will be more*, according to sources within the financial world. Based on my findings, these are not mere random, tragic cases of suicide, but of the methodical silencing of individuals who had the ability to expose financial fraud at the highest levels, and the complicity of certain governmental agencies and individuals who are engaged in the greatest theft of wealth the world has ever seen." He goes on to state, "One must look back far enough to understand the enormity of the lie and the criminality of bankers and

---

[209] http://www.forbes.com/sites/ralphbenko/2013/03/11/1-6-billion-rounds-of-ammo-for-homeland-security-its-time-for-a-national-conversation/

[210] http://en.wikipedia.org/wiki/United_States_Secretary_of_Homeland_Security

governments alike. We must understand the legal restraints that were severed during the Clinton years and the congress that changed the rules regarding financial institutions. We must understand that the criminal acts were bold and bipartisan, and were designed to consolidate wealth through the destruction of the middle class. All of this is part of a much larger plan to establish a one world economy by "killing" the U.S. dollar and consequently, eradicating the middle class by a cabal of globalists that existed and continue to exist within all sectors of our government. The results will be crippling to not just the United States, but the entire Western world." [211] There is much motive revealed here!

Without a doubt, it will cause chaos and is the perfect opportunity for the government to call for a "state of emergency," where the already prepared military, including foreign troops, and most local police departments will begin to carry out martial law. This could potentially include the use of the FEMA camps mentioned many times and any citizens who are seen as tyrants, not complying with the government, could be detained without question under the National Defense Authorization Act. If we could rewind a bit to the interview by Jack Chick of the former Jesuit, Alberto Rivera, who warned us of the purposeful creation of chaos resulting in anarchy and the final takeover of the United States, could this be that it is finally coming to fulfillment?

Now, this chapter was presented as a court case and I have given mountains of evidence against the accused, which are the Jesuits and the Roman Catholic Church. In my closing argument, I would like to state that based on the evidence presented, I truly believe that there has been a conspiracy to destroy the United States of America from the inside-out since its inception as a nation. I believe that this great country represented a place of refuge for those attempting to escape the iron fist of Rome. But, through deceit and mental warfare, the Jesuits have slowly secured a Roman Catholic majority here in the United States, making it possible to completely control the financial and judicial status of our nation. This has not happened overnight, but by careful engineering as I have attempted to prove. As a juror, how do you see the defendant? Based on the evidence presented, would you vote guilty or non-guilty?

---

[211] http://www.homelandsecurityus.com/archives/10482

Chapter Twelve

WAKE UP CALL!

The title of this book, *While Men Slept*, was chosen because I ultimately feel like the people of America have allowed this nation to fall prey to the enemy while men were lethargically sleeping. God warned us in **1 Peter 5:8** to **"Be sober, be vigilant; because your adversary the Devil, as a roaring lion, walks about seeking whom he may devour."** The Scripture inspiration used for the title of the book speaks of what transpired *while men slept* and that **"His enemy came and sowed tares among the wheat, and went his way (Matthew 13:25)."** Jesus exposes the enemy precisely and tells us in **Matthew 13:38-39** that **"the tares are children of the wicked one; The enemy that sowed them is the devil."** It is so obvious that this sowing of the tares by the enemy was *intentional*, and the purpose was to destroy the harvest. The parallels between everything that has been written in this manuscript about the Jesuit Order and their goal to set up the Antichrist system of Satan worship and the purpose of the enemy in this Scripture in Matthew are just too seamless.

But, while the enemy has a plan, God is ultimately in control and will only allow the enemy's plan to go forth when He is ready. I also know that the Gospel of Jesus Christ is being preached all over the world through ministries called by God in these last days and supported by the remnant of believers who want to see people saved by the blood of

Jesus Christ. We also have God ordained missionaries who work tirelessly to see souls brought to the saving knowledge of Jesus Christ. I truly believe that God is giving man a last chance here to accept the offering of His only Son, Jesus, as the means of Eternal Life. The Bible speaks of a great "catching away **(1Thessalonians 4:16-17)**" of the Saints in Christ and then a period of **"great tribulation (Matthew 24:21),"** which will be worse than anything ever conceived on this Earth thus far. I realize that people will have an opportunity to be saved during the "Great Tribulation," but it will be a most difficult time to be a true Christian because of the persecution of the Antichrist system.

Will the plan of the Satan win in the end and will he defeat the plan of God? The Bible clearly says, "No!" In **Revelation 17:3**, it speaks of a woman, called **"the whore"** who rides on the back of the beast, which is the Antichrist system. **Revelation 17: 4-6** describes this woman where it states, **"And the woman was arrayed in purple and scarlet colour, and decked with gold and precious stones and pearls, having a golden cup in her hand full of abominations and filthiness of her fornication. And upon her forehead was a name written, MYSTERY, BABYLON THE GREAT, THE MOTHER OF HARLOTS AND ABOMINATIONS OF THE EARTH. And I saw the woman drunken with the blood of the Saints, and with the blood of the martyrs of Jesus . . ."** As previously revealed, the Roman Catholic Church *is* "**MYSTERY BABYLON**" and she *is* the **"MOTHER OF HARLOTS."** She has acquired immeasurable wealth over the centuries through the sale of indulgences, where family members paid the Roman Catholic Church so that their deceased loved ones would spend less time in her fictitious place called "purgatory"; and also from the many inquisitions where the money and land of the dead "heretics" went directly into the pope's bloody hands.

Many prophecy scholars ascertain that **"the woman/whore"** of **Revelation 17** is the one world religious system under the false prophet and the Antichrist which is yet to come. I do agree with this statement and do not think that it contradicts the fact that I believe that **"the woman/whore"** is the Church of Rome. There *will be* an end time one world religion and I believe that the pope of Rome and the Roman Catholic Church will be key in this scenario, as I have already shown.

Why do I believe this? Because the preparation for the New World Order religious system has been paved by the *Ecumenical Movement* which was spearheaded by Pope John Paul II and has continued to gain acceptance under Pope Benedict XVI. Benedict XVI even told the Muslims that "religious dialogue and inner-cultural dialogue are necessary to build a world of peace." He said, "Christians and Muslims must learn to work together . . . in order to guard against all forms of intolerance and to oppose all manifestations of violence."[212] And of course, Pope Francis I is the most ecumenically minded pope who has ever been elected!

The religious system taking shape under Pope Francis right now very likely will incorporate all major religions into one system of theology without actually changing their individual basic belief systems. It will basically be a world system of *religious tolerance*. More and more, we are convinced by the media and press that the root cause for most war, bloodshed and injustice is religious intolerance. So, "tolerance" is the New Age—one world gospel of hope today. More and more any religious group which is viewed as intolerant, like true Christianity, is *becoming less tolerated!* True Christianity, because of its unyielding stand of Salvation in Jesus Christ alone based on the Word of God, is being labeled as intolerant and fanatical.

Revelation 17:1 says **"Come hither; I will show unto you the Judgment of the *great whore* who sits upon many waters: With whom the kings of the earth have committed fornication, and the inhabitants of the earth have been made drunk with the wine of her fornication."** The whole world has been deceived by her in one form or another; either through the spiritual or political deception. Does God clearly reveal the identity of **"the whore"**? I believe He does in **Revelation 17:9** where it states, **"And here is the mind which has wisdom. The seven heads are seven mountains, on which the woman sits."** The seven heads mentioned here are referring to the seven heads with ten horns found on the beast in **Revelation 17:3**. I believe that the seven mountains or hills which the woman sits upon represent Rome, which for the last 2000 years has been known as "a city on seven

---

212   http://www.thedailynewsegypt.com/article.aspx?ArticleID=3145

hills."[213] Then later in **Revelation 17:18** it says, **"And the woman which you saw *is that great city,* which reigns over the kings of the earth** (my italics)." Basically, these two verses solidify that the woman riding on the back of the beast is the city of Rome; where Vatican City, the headquarters of the papacy, is located. The *Catholic Encyclopedia* states, "It is within the city of Rome, called the city of seven hills, that the entire area of Vatican State proper is now confined."[214]

I personally believe that the word **"mystery"** separates *spiritual* Babylon from *literal* Babylon. What will happen to this city called **"MYSTERY, BABYLON THE GREAT"** according to the Word of God? The Bible states in **Jeremiah 51: 8, 62-64** that Babylon will be destroyed when it says, **"Babylon is suddenly fallen and destroyed . . . And it shall be, when you have made an end of reading this Book, that you shall bind a stone to it, and cast it into the midst of Euphrates: And you shall say, Thus shall Babylon sink, and *shall not rise* from the evil that I will bring upon her . . . (my italics)"** Then in **Revelation 14:8** it says, **"And there followed another Angel, saying, Babylon is fallen, is fallen, that great city, because she made all nations drink of the wine of wrath of her fornication."** Once again in **Revelation 18:2-3, 8, 21** it says, **"And he cried mightily with a strong voice saying, Babylon the great is fallen, is fallen, and is become the habitation of devils, and the hold of every unclean and hateful bird. For all nations have drunk of the wine of the wrath of her fornication, and the kings of the earth have committed fornication with her . . . and she shall be utterly burned with fire: for strong is the Lord God Who judges her . . . And a mighty Angel took up a stone like a great millstone, and cast it into the sea, saying, Thus with violence shall that great city Babylon be thrown down, and shall be found no more at all."** It couldn't be any clearer that **"BABYLON THE GREAT,"** which is the Roman Catholic Church's pagan system of worship, will be utterly destroyed by fire and cast into the sea, *never, ever to be revived again.*

---

[213] *A Woman Rides the Beast,* Dave Hunt, Harvest House Publishers, Oregon, 1994, page 67

[214] *The Catholic Encyclopedia,* (Thomas Nelson, 1976) "Rome"

But, who will God use to destroy **"the whore"** of **Revelation 17?** **Revelation 17:16** says, **"And the ten horns which you saw upon the beast, these shall hate the whore** (The Roman Catholic Church)**, and shall make her desolate and naked, and shall eat her flesh, and burn her with fire."** The ten horns represent the ten nation confederations or the ten toes on the statue of which King Nebuchadnezzar dreamed. These ten nations will turn on **"the whore"** and burn her with fire. Do you recall what a now born-again believer, Gerard Bouffard, who was a former Bishop and high-ranking Vatican official *and* assistant to Pope John Paul II said about the Jesuits? He stated, "I know firsthand that the Vatican controls and monitors everything in Israel with the intention of destroying the Jews. The true purpose of the Jesuit Order is to orchestrate and control all leaders of the world in order to bring about a major worldwide conflict which will eventually destroy America, the Middle East and Israel. They destroy everything from within and *want to bring about the destruction of the Catholic Church*, as well, in order to usher in a *one world religion based on Satanism* (my italics)."[215] While the satanic Jesuits have used the Roman Catholic Church to gain immeasurable power, they ultimately will have no use for her in the end. Once their plan of world dominance is in place, they will utterly destroy her by fire and set up their satanic religious system! Of course, the story does not end there, because the Bible is clear that Jesus Christ will come back at His second coming and destroy Antichrist at the Battle of Armageddon, making God the ultimate victor **(Revelation 16:16, 19:11-21)!**

The pagan religious system of Babylon has never disappeared! This system of worship was created by Satan himself, and it was spread all over the world at the dispersion of the people from the Tower of Babel. While this false religion has transformed into many different names, underneath it all is the worship of another god or gods, namely Satan or Lucifer. But in God's Word, we can also see how the Tower of Babel was to be revived once again under a universal religious system and a New World Order with one person as the sole head. This person will be Antichrist and his "side-kick" will be the false prophet who will head the one world religious system. We also can see how God will utterly destroy the Babylonian system once and for all!

---

[215] http://www.spirittruth.com/view/?pageID=73185

This is your "WAKE UP CALL" just in case you have slept through this destructive plan of the enemy and were oblivious to it prior to reading the details presented in this book. Jesus differentiates between two types of people in the following Scripture and I think it is important to know exactly where you stand in the grand scheme of things: are you alert and sold out to Jesus Christ or are you sleeping and deaf to His warnings? In **Matthew 13:10-17** the Disciples asked Jesus why He spoke in parables, and Jesus answered them saying, **"Because it is given unto you to know the mysteries of the Kingdom of Heaven, but to them it is not given** (speaking of those who have no concern). **For whosoever has, to him shall be given, and he shall have more abundance: but whosoever has not, from him shall be taken away even that he has. Therefore speak I to them in parables: because they seeing see not; and hearing they hear not, neither do they understand. And in them is fulfilled the Prophecy of Isaiah, which says, By hearing ye shall hear, and shall not understand; and seeing ye shall see, and not perceive.** *For his people's heart is waxed gross, and their ears are dull of hearing, and their eyes they have closed;* **lest at any time they should see with their eyes, and hear with their ears, and should understand with their heart, and should be converted, and I should heal them. But blessed are your eyes, for they see: and your ears, for they hear. For verily I say unto you, That many Prophets and righteous men have desired to see those things which ye see, and have not seen them; and to hear those things which you hear, and have not heard them** (my italics)." Can you *see* and can you *hear* what the Spirit of the Lord has been trying to show you? *Jesus Christ is your one and only hope to escape the wrath to come. Wake up and trust in Him today and no matter what the enemy has planned, you have the assurance of Eternal Life in Heaven which is promised in God's Holy Word!* MARANATHA . . . Come quickly Lord Jesus!

LIST OF FEMA CAMPS
LOCATED IN THE U.S.[216]

ALABAMA

Opelika—Military compound either in or very near town

Aliceville—WWII German POW camp; capacity 15,000

Ft. McClellan (Anniston)—Opposite side of town from Army Depot

Maxwell AFB (Montgomery)—Civilian prison camp established under Operation Garden Plot, currently operating with support staff and small inmate population

Talladega—Federal prison "satellite" camp

ALASKA

Wilderness—East of Anchorage. No roads, Air & Railroad access only; estimated capacity of 500,000

Elmendorf AFB—Northeast area of Anchorage—far end of base. Garden Plot facility

Eielson AFB—Southeast of Fairbanks. Operation Garden Plot facility

Ft. Wainwright—East of Fairbanks

ARIZONA

Ft. Huachuca—20 miles from Mexican border, 30 miles from Nogales Rex '84 facility.

Pinal County—on the Gila River—WWII Japanese detention camp; may be renovated

Yuma County—Colorado River—Site of former Japanese detention camp (near proving grounds); this site was completely removed in 1990 according to some reports

Phoenix—Federal Prison Satellite Camp; main federal facility expanded

Florence—WWII prison camp *now renovated and operational* with staff & 400 prisoners; capacity of 3,500

[216] SOURCE: http://www.thedailysheeple.com/find-the-fema-camp-nearest-you_062013

Wickenburg—Airport is ready for conversion; total capacity unknown

Davis-Monthan AFB (Tucson)—Fully staffed and presently holding prisoners

Sedona—site of possible UN base

ARKANSAS

Ft. Chaffee (near Fort Smith, Arkansas)—Has new runway for aircraft, new camp facility with cap of 40,000 prisoners

***Pine Bluff Arsenal*—This location also is the repository for B-Z nerve agent, which causes sleepiness, dizziness, stupor; admitted use is for civilian control

Jerome—Chicot/Drew Counties—site of WWII Japanese camps

***Rohwer Descha County*—site of WWII Japanese camps

***Blythville AFB*—Closed airbase now being used as camp; new wooden barracks have been constructed at this location, classic decorations: guard towers, barbed wire high fences

Berryville—FEMA facility located east of Eureka Springs off Hwy. 62

Omaha—Northeast of Berryville near Missouri state line, on Hwy 65 south of old wood processing plant; possible crematory facility

CALIFORNIA

***Vandenburg AFB*—Rex 84 facility, located near Lompoc & Santa Maria; Internment facility located near the oceanside, close to Space Launch Complex #6, also called "Slick Six"; the launch site has had "a flawless failure record" and is rarely used

***Norton AFB*—(closed base) now staffed with UN according to some sources Tule Lake—area of "wildlife refuge", accessible by unpaved road, just inside Modoc County

Fort Ord—Closed in 1994, this facility is now an urban warfare training center for US and foreign troops and may have some "P.O.W.—C.I." enclosures

***Twentynine Palms Marine Base*—Birthplace of the infamous "Would you shoot American citizens?" Quiz; new camps being built on "back 40".

Oakdale—Rex 84 camp capable of holding at least 20,000 people. 90 mi. East of San Francisco

Terminal Island—(Long Beach) located next to naval shipyards operated by ChiCom shipping interests; federal prison facility located here; possible deportation point

Ft. Irwin—FEMA facility near Barstow; base is designated inactive but has staffed camp

McClellan AFB—facility capable for 30,000-35,000

Sacramento Army Depot—No specific information at this time

Mather AFB—Road to facility is blocked off by cement barriers and a stop sign, sign states area is restricted; as of 1997 there were barbed wire fences pointing inward, a row of stadium lights pointed toward an empty field, etc. Black boxes on poles may have been cameras

COLORADO
Trinidad—WWII German/Italian camp being renovated

Granada—Prowers County—WWII Japanese internment camp

Ft. Carson—Along route 115 near Canon City

CONNECTICUT
No data available

DELAWARE
No data available

FLORIDA
Avon Park—Air Force gunnery range, Avon Park has an on-base "correctional facility" which was a former WWII detention camp

Camp Krome—DoJ detention/interrogation center, Rex 84 facility

Eglin AFB—This base is over 30 miles long, from Pensacola to Hwy 331 in De Funiak Springs; high capacity facility, presently manned and populated with some prisoners

Pensacola—Federal Prison Camp Everglades—It is believed that a facility may be carved out of the wilds here

GEORGIA
Ft. Benning—Located east of Columbus near Alabama state line; Rex 84 site, prisoners brought in via Lawson Army airfield

Ft. Mc Pherson—US Force Command—Multiple reports that this will be the national headquarters and coordinating center for foreign/ UN troop movement and detainee collection

Ft. Gordon—West of Augusta—No information at this time

Unadilla—Dooly County—Manned, staffed FEMA prison on route 230, no prisoners

Oglethorpe—Macon County; facility is located five miles from Montezuma, three miles from Oglethorpe. This FEMA prison has no staff and no prisoners

Morgan—Calhoun County, FEMA facility is fully manned & staffed— no prisoners

Camilla—Mitchell County, south of Albany. This FEMA facility is located on Mt. Zion Rd approximately 5.7 miles south of Camilla. Unmanned—no prisoners, no staff

Hawkinsville—Wilcox County; Five miles east of town, fully manned and staffed but no prisoners. Located on fire road 100/Upper River Road

Abbeville—South of Hawkinsville on US route 129; south of town off route 280 near Ocmulgee River. FEMA facility is staffed but without prisoners

McRae—Telfair County—1.5 miles west of McRae on Hwy 134 (8th St); facility is on Irwinton Avenue off 8th St., manned & staffed—no prisoners

Fort Gillem—South side of Atlanta—FEMA designated detention facility

Fort Stewart—Savannah area—FEMA designated detention facility

HAWAII

Halawa Heights—Crematory facility located in hills above city. Area is marked as a state department of health laboratory

Barbers Point NAS—There are several military areas that could be equipped for detention / deportation

Honolulu—Detention transfer facility at the Honolulu airport similar in construction to the one in Oklahoma (pentagon-shaped building where airplanes can taxi up to)

IDAHO

Minidoka/Jerome Counties—WWII Japanese-American internment facility possibly under renovation

Clearwater National Forest—Near Lolo Pass—Just miles from the Montana state line near Moose Creek, this unmanned facility is reported to have a nearby airfield

Wilderness areas—Possible location. No data.

ILLINOIS

Marseilles—Located on the Illinois River off Interstate 80 on Hwy 6. It is a relatively small facility with a cap of 1400 prisoners. Though it is small it is designed like prison facilities with barred windows, but the real smoking gun is the presence of military vehicles. Being located on the Illinois River it is possible that prisoners will be brought in by water as well as by road and air. This facility is approximately 75 miles west of Chicago. National Guard training area nearby

Scott AFB—Barbed wire prisoner enclosure reported to exist just off-base. More info needed, as another facility on-base is believed to exist

Pekin—This Federal satellite prison camp is also on the Illinois River, just south of Peoria. It supplements the federal penitentiary in Marion, which is equipped to handle additional population outside on the grounds

Chanute AFB—Rantoul, near Champaign/Urbana—This closed base had WWII—era barracks that were condemned and torn down, but the medical facility was upgraded and additional fencing put up in the area

Marion—Federal Penitentiary and satellite prison camp inside Crab Orchard Nat'l Wildlife Refuge. Manned, staffed, populated fully

Greenfield—Two federal correctional "satellite prison camps" serving Marion—populated as above

Shawnee National Forest—Pope County—This area has seen heavy traffic of foreign military equipment and troops via Illinois Central Railroad, which runs through the area. Suspected location is unknown, but may be close to Vienna and Shawnee correctional centers, located 6 mi. west of Dixon Springs

Savanna Army Depot—NW area of state on Mississippi River

Lincoln, Sheridan, Menard, Pontiac, Galesburg—State prison facilities equipped for major expansion and close or adjacent to highways & railroad tracks

Kankakee—Abandoned industrial area on west side of town (Rt.17 & Main) designated as FEMA detention site. Equipped with water tower, incinerator, a small train yard behind it and the rear of the facility is surrounded by barbed wire facing inwards.

INDIANA

Indianapolis / Marion County—Amtrak railcar repair facility (closed); controversial site of a major alleged detention / processing center. Although some sources state that this site is a "red herring", photographic and video evidence suggests otherwise. This large facility contains large 3-4 inch gas mains to large furnaces (crematoria), helicopter landing pads, railheads for prisoners, Red/Blue/Green zones for classifying/processing incoming personnel, one-way turnstiles, barracks, towers, high fences with razor wire, etc. Personnel with government clearance who are friendly to the patriot movement took a guided tour of the facility to confirm this site. This site is located next to a closed refrigeration plant facility

Ft. Benjamin Harrison—Located in the northeast part of Indianapolis, this base has been decommissioned from "active" use but portions are still ideally converted to hold detainees. Helicopter landing areas still exist for prisoners to be brought in by air, land & rail

Crown Point—Across street from county jail, former hospital. One wing presently being used for county work-release program, 80% of facility still unused. Possible FEMA detention center or holding facility

Camp Atterbury—Facility is converted to hold prisoners and boasts two active compounds presently configured for minimum security detainees. Located just west of Interstate 65 near Edinburgh, south of Indianapolis.

Terre Haute—Federal Correctional Institution, Satellite prison camp and death facility. Equipped with crematoria reported to have a capacity of 3,000 people a day. FEMA designated facility located her

Fort Wayne—This city located in Northeast Indiana has a FEMA designated detention facility, accessible by air, road and nearby rail

Kingsbury—This "closed" military base is adjacent to a state fish & wildlife preserve. Part of the base is converted to an industrial park, but the southern portion of this property is still used. It is bordered on the south by railroad, and is staffed with some foreign-speaking UN troops. A local police officer who was hunting and camping close to the base in the game preserve was accosted, roughed up, and warned by the English-speaking unit commander to stay away from the area. It was suggested to the officer that the welfare of his family would depend on his "silence". Located just southeast of LaPorte

Jasper-Pulaski Wildlife Area—Youth Corrections farm located here. Facility is "closed", but is still staffed and being "renovated". Total capacity unknown

Grissom AFB—This closed airbase still handles a lot of traffic, and has a "state-owned" prison compound on the southern part of the facility.

UNICOR

Jefferson Proving Grounds—Southern Indiana—This facility was an active base with test firing occurring daily. Portions of the base have been opened to create an industrial park, but other areas are still highly restricted. A camp is believed to be located "downrange". Facility is equipped with an airfield and has a nearby rail line

Newport Army Depot—VX nerve gas storage facility. Secret meetings were held here in 1998 regarding the addition of the Kankakee River watershed to the Heritage Rivers Initiative

Hammond—large enclosure identified in FEMA-designated city.

IOWA

No data available.

KANSAS

Leavenworth—US Marshal's Fed Holding Facility, US Penitentiary, Federal Prison Camp, McConnell Air Force Base. Federal death penalty facility

Concordia—WWII German POW camp used to exist at this location but there is no facility there at this time

Ft. Riley—Just north of Interstate 70, airport, near city of Manhattan

El Dorado—Federal prison converted into forced-labor camp, UNICOR industries

Topeka—80 acres has been converted into a temporary holding camp.

KENTUCKY

Ashland—Federal prison camp in Eastern Kentucky near the Ohio River

Louisville—FEMA detention facility, located near restricted area US naval ordnance plant. Military airfield located at facility, which is on south side of city

Lexington—FEMA detention facility, National Guard base with adjacent airport facility

Manchester—Federal prison camp located inside Dan Boone National Forest

Ft. Knox—Detention center, possibly located near Salt River, in restricted area of base. Local patriots advise that black Special Forces & UN gray helicopters are occasionally seen in area

Land Between the Lakes—This area was declared a UN biosphere and is an ideal geographic location for detention facilities. Area is an isthmus extending out from Tennessee, between Lake Barkley on the east and Kentucky Lake on the west. Just scant miles from Fort Campbell in Tennessee

LOUISIANA

Ft. Polk—This is a main base for UN troops and personnel, as well as, a training center for the disarmament of America

Livingston—WWII German/Italian internment camp being renovated; halfway between Baton Rouge and Hammond, several miles north of Interstate 12

Oakdale—Located on US route 165 about 50 miles south of Alexandria; two federal detention centers just southeast of Fort Polk

MAINE

Houlton—WWII German internment camp in Northern Maine, off US Route 1

MARYLAND, and DC

Ft. Meade—Halfway between the District of Criminals and Baltimore

Ft. Detrick—Biological warfare center for the NWO, located in Frederick

MASSACHUSETTS

Camp Edwards / Otis AFB—Cape Cod—This "inactive" base is being converted to hold many New Englander patriots. Capacity unknown

Ft. Devens—Active detention facility

MICHIGAN

Camp Grayling—Michigan National Guard base has several confirmed detention camps, classic setup with high fences, razor wire, etc. Guard towers are very well-built. Multiple compounds within larger enclosures. Facility deep within forest area

Sawyer AFB—Upper Peninsula—south of Marquette—No data available

Bay City—Classic enclosure with guard towers, high fence, and close to shipping port on Saginaw Bay, which connects to Lake Huron. Could be a deportation point to overseas via St. Lawrence Seaway

Southwest—possibly Berrien County—FEMA detention center

Lansing—FEMA detention facility

MINNESOTA

Duluth—Federal prison camp facility

Camp Ripley—new prison facility

MISSISSIPPI

No data available

MISSOURI

Richards-Gebaur AFB—located in Grandview, near K.C.MO. A very large internment facility has been built on this base, and all base personnel are restricted from coming near it

Ft. Leonard Wood—Situated in the middle of Mark Twain National Forest in Pulaski County. This site has been known for some UN training, also home to the US Army Urban Warfare Training school "Stem Village"

Warsaw—Unconfirmed report of a large concentration camp facility

MONTANA
Malmstrom AFB—UN aircraft groups stationed here, and possibly a detention facility

NEBRASKA
Scottsbluff—WWII German POW camp (renovated?)
Northwest, Northeast corners of state—FEMA detention facilities—more data needed
South Central part of state—Many old WWII sites—some may be renovated

NEVADA
Elko—Ten miles south of town
Wells—Camp is located in the O'Niel basin area, 40 miles north of Wells, past Thousand Springs, west off Hwy 93 for 25 miles
Pershing County—Camp is located at I-80 mile marker 112, south side of the highway, about a mile back on the county road and then just off the road about 3/4mi
Winnemucca—Battle Mountain area—at the base of the mountains. Nellis
Air Force Range—Northwest from Las Vegas on Route 95
Nellis AFB—just north of Las Vegas on Hwy 604
Stillwater Naval Air Station—east of Reno. No additional data

NEW HAMPSHIRE / VERMONT
Northern New Hampshire—near Lake Francis. No additional data

NEW JERSEY
Ft. Dix / McGuire AFB—Possible deportation point for detainees. Lots of pictures taken of detention compounds and posted on Internet, this camp is well-known. Facility is now complete and ready for occupancy

NEW MEXICO
Ft. Bliss—This base actually straddles the Texas state line just south of Alomogordo; encompasses thousands of acres

Holloman AFB (Alomogordo)—Home of the German Luftwaffe in Amerika; major UN base. New facility being built on this base, according to recent visitors. Many former USAF buildings have been torn down by the busy and rapidly growing German military force located here

Fort Stanton—currently being used as a youth detention facility approximately 35 miles north of Ruidoso, New Mexico. Not a great deal of information concerning the Lordsburg location

White Sands Missile Range—Currently being used as a storage facility for United Nations vehicles and equipment. Observers have seen this material brought in on the Whitesands rail spur in Oro Grande New Mexico about thirty miles from the Texas, New Mexico Border

NEW YORK

Ft. Drum—two compounds: Rex 84 detention camp and FEMA detention facility

Albany—FEMA detention facility

Otisville—Federal correctional facility, near Middletown

Buffalo—FEMA detention facility

NORTH CAROLINA

Camp Lejeune / New River Marine Airfield—facility has renovated, occupied WWII detention compounds and "mock city" that closely resembles Anytown, USA

Fort Bragg—Special Warfare Training Center. Renovated WWII detention facility

Andrews—Federal experiment in putting a small town under siege. Began with the search/ hunt for survivalist Eric Rudolph. No persons were allowed in or out of town without federal permission and travel through town was highly restricted. Most residents compelled to stay in their homes. Unregistered Baptist pastor from Indiana visiting Andrews affirmed these facts

NORTH DAKOTA

Minot AFB—Home of UN air group. More data needed on facility

OHIO
Camp Perry—Site renovated; once used as a POW camp to house German and Italian prisoners of WWII. Some tar paper covered huts built for housing these prisoners are still standing. Recently, the construction of multiple 200-man barracks have replaced most of the huts

Cincinnati, Cleveland, Columbus—FEMA detention facilities

Lima—FEMA detention facility. Another facility located in/near old stone quarry near Interstate 75. Railroad access to property and fences

OKLAHOMA
Tinker AFB (OKC)—All base personnel are prohibited from going near civilian detention area, which is under constant guard

Will Rogers World Airport—FEMA's main processing center for west of the Mississippi. All personnel are kept out of the security zone. Federal prisoner transfer center located here (A pentagon-shaped building where airplanes can taxi up to). Photos have been taken and this site will try to post soon!

El Reno—Renovated federal internment facility with CURRENT population of 12,000 on Route 66

McAlester—near Army Munitions Plant property—former WWII German / Italian POW camp designated for future use

Ft. Sill (Lawton)—Former WWII detention camps. More data still needed

OREGON
Sheridan—Federal prison satellite camp northwest of Salem

Josephine County—WWII Japanese internment camp ready for renovation

Sheridan—FEMA detention center

Umatilla—New prison spotted

PENNSYLVANIA
Allenwood—Federal prison camp located south of Williamsport on the Susquehanna River. It has a current inmate population of 300, and is identified by William Pabst as having a capacity in excess of 15,000 on 400 acres

Indiantown Gap Military Reservation—located north of Harrisburg. Used for WWII POW camp and renovated by Jimmy Carter. Was used to hold Cubans during Mariel boat lift

Camp Hill—State prison close to Army depot. Lots of room, located in Camp Hill, PA

New Cumberland Army Depot—on the Susquehanna River, located off Interstate 83 and Interstate 76

Schuylkill Haven—Federal prison camp, north of Reading

SOUTH CAROLINA

Greenville—Unoccupied youth prison camp; total capacity unknown

Charleston—Naval Reserve & Air Force base, restricted area on naval base

SOUTH DAKOTA

Yankton—Federal prison camp

Black Hills National Forest—north of Edgemont, southwest part of state; WWII internment camp being renovated

TENNESSEE

Ft. Campbell—Next to Land Between the Lakes; adjacent to airfield and US Alt. 41

Millington—Federal prison camp next door to Memphis Naval Air Station

Crossville—Site of WWII German / Italian prison camp is renovated; completed barracks and behind the camp in the woods is a training facility with high tight ropes and a rappelling deck

Nashville—There are two buildings built on State property that are definitely built to hold prisoners. They are identical buildings—side by side on Old Briley Parkway. High barbed wire fence that curves inward.

TEXAS

Austin—Robert Mueller Municipal airport has detention areas inside hangars

Bastrop—Prison and military vehicle motor pool

Eden—1500 bed privately run federal center. Currently holds illegal aliens

Ft. Hood (Killeen)—Newly built concentration camp, with towers, barbed wire etc., just like the one featured in the movie Amerika.

Mock city for NWO shock—force training. Some footage of this area was used in "Waco: A New Revelation"

Reese AFB (Lubbock)—FEMA designated detention facility

Sheppard AFB—in Wichita Falls just south of Ft. Sill, OK. FEMA designated detention facility

North Dallas—near Carrolton—water treatment plant, close to interstate and railroad

Mexia—East of Waco 33mi.; WWII German facility may be renovated

Amarillo—FEMA designated detention facility

Ft. Bliss (El Paso)—Extensive renovation of buildings and from what patriots have been able to see, many of these buildings that are being renovated are being surrounded by razor wire

Beaumont / Port Arthur area—hundreds of acres of federal camps already built on large-scale detention camp design, complete with the double rows of chain link fencing with razor type concertina wire on top of each row. Some (but not all) of these facilities are currently being used for low-risk state prisoners who require a minimum of supervision

Ft. Worth—Federal prison under construction on the site of Carswell AFB

UTAH

Millard County—Central Utah—WWII Japanese camp. (Renovated?)

Ft. Douglas—This "inactive" military reservation has a renovated WWII concentration camp

Migratory Bird Refuge—West of Brigham City—contains a WWII internment camp that was built before the game preserve was established

Cedar City—east of city—no data available

Wendover—WWII internment camp may be renovated.

Skull Valley—southwestern Camp William property—east of the old bombing range. Camp was accidentally discovered by a man and his son who were rabbit hunting; they were discovered and apprehended. SW of Tooele.

VIRGINIA

Ft. A.P. Hill (Fredericksburg)—Rex 84/ FEMA facility; estimated capacity 45,000

Petersburg—Federal satellite prison camp, south of Richmond.

WEST VIRGINIA
Beckley—Alderson—Lewisburg—Former WWII detention camps that are now converted into active federal prison complexes capable of holding several times their current populations. Alderson is presently a women's federal reformatory

Morgantown—Federal prison camp located in northern WV; just north of Kingwood

Mill Creek—FEMA detention facility

Kingwood—Newly built detention camp at Camp Dawson Army Reservation

WASHINGTON
Seattle/Tacoma—SeaTac Airport: fully operational federal transfer center

Okanogan County—Borders Canada and is a site for a massive concentration camp capable of holding hundreds of thousands of people for slave labor. This is probably one of the locations that will be used to hold hard core patriots who will be held captive for the rest of their lives

Sand Point Naval Station—Seattle—FEMA detention center used actively during the 1999 WTO protests to classify prisoners

Ft. Lewis / McChord AFB—near Tacoma—This is one of several sites that may be used to ship prisoners overseas for slave labor

WISCONSIN
Ft. McCoy—Rex 84 facility with several complete interment compounds

Oxford—Central part of state—Federal prison & satellite camp and FEMA detention facility

WYOMING
Heart Mountain—Park County N. of Cody—WWII Japanese internment camp ready for renovation

Laramie—FEMA detention facility

Southwest—near Lyman—FEMA detention facility

East Yellowstone—Manned internment facility—Investigating patriots were apprehended by European soldiers speaking in an unknown language. Federal government assumed custody of the persons and arranged their release.

About the Author

I spent 32 years in the Roman Catholic religious system which claimed that I had to work my way to Heaven, but I never truly understood this religion which I had been baptized into at only 10 days old. When I finally broke free and became a "new creation" in Christ Jesus in 2005, the Lord began to open up to me the closet of skeletons that my religion had been hiding. The burden became so great for the salvation of souls that I felt compelled to write my first book entitled, *What I Would Tell You, If You Would Listen*. After writing it, I vowed to never write another book, but apparently God had different plans! One morning in reading God's Word, He spoke to me a title and two months later I had a fully edited manuscript. That book, *Men Rule . . . But God Overrules* is an awakening to the reality of what is going on in this world today spiritually and politically. It reveals the sinister plotting of Satan to use men of this world to carry out his wicked plans. I did not publicize the book at all, but when Jorge Bergoglio, the first Jesuit pope to be elected, took the papal throne in March of 2013, I felt an urgency to warn people about the plan of the enemy.

This latest book, *While Men Slept*, is a result of watching the Church world, especially in America, being inundated with false doctrine and a watered down, social gospel which has created an apathetic race of people who no longer live holy and do not feel it necessary to share the Gospel of Jesus Christ with others. Knowing that the enemy had intentionally introduced this social gospel and promised the destruction of America, I could not rest until the truth was revealed. After God dealt with me for months about writing this, I could no longer ignore Him when He told me in **Jeremiah 50:2, "Declare ye among the nations, and publish, and set up a standard; publish, and conceal not."** I am also a former educator and there is no better lesson than educating people about what Jesus accomplished for us on the Cross of Calvary; defeating Satan, death and Hell! I currently reside in the heart of the Cajun Country in South Louisiana with my husband and two children. I continue to research and write while also working as a photographer specializing in family, children and senior portraits.

Karen

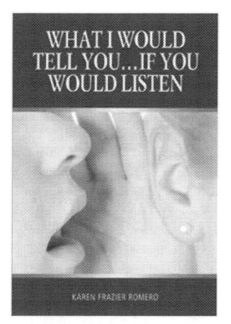